"The cross of Jesus Christ is cent
many views of what the cross acc
Here is a fascinating dialogue l
scholars who range throughout the Scriptures, presenting
their views of the significance of the atonement—the death of
Jesus Christ. Wright and Gathercole question each other, and
they respond to questions from their audience. Their stimu-
lating discussion opens wide areas to contemplate as we see
their paths converge and diverge from each other. Important
insights emerge here. So do deeper perceptions of what the
cross can mean, theologically and personally."
　　　　　—Donald K. McKim, former Academic Dean
　　　　　　　　　and Professor of Theology,
　　　　　　　　　Memphis Theological Seminary

"Reading this enthralling book deepens and remolds our understanding of the cross of Jesus. Wright's holistic atonement is truly
enlightening, Gathercole's substitutionary atonement is thought
provoking, and Stewart's view of the Lord's Supper is enriching.
This book must be read by all Christians who tussle with different atonement theories."
　　　　　—Andrew S. Park, author of *Triune Atonement*
　　　　　　　　　and Professor of Theology and Ethics,
　　　　　　　　　United Theological Seminary

"Jesus' death bears many meanings in Scripture and Christian
interpretation, including the defeat of Satan, forgiveness of sins,
demonstration of love, creation of community, sign of solidar-
ity, and start of the eschaton. In this book, eminent scholars
N. T. Wright and Simon Gathercole—having already written
books on Christ's cross—speak, spout, split, and specify these
many meanings in amazing ways. Enlivened by queries from
the floor, their conversation concludes without closure, and

yet this slender volume offers entrée into today's atonement debates. Stewart's introduction and concluding bibliography further enhance its value as a starting point for those just dipping their toes into the ocean of literature on Jesus' death."

—Michael McClymond,
Professor of Modern Christianity,
Saint Louis University

"This heady conversation among serious theologians who are good humored, agile, and erudite is a model for how the church thinks. The topic of atonement remains a mystery beyond formulation, which, of course, is why the church has never pronounced definitively on the theme. In the meantime, the pondering of these theologians lets us see (1) how faithful thinking is done, (2) how thick the claim of Christ is, and (3) how serious, generous interpretation is generative of new possibility. This is a welcome conversation that sketches out imaginative scenarios for future work. The practice of this book is one of deep faith and bold thinking, just what the church must now undertake in fresh ways."

—Walter Brueggemann, William Marcellus McPheeters
Professor Emeritus of Old Testament,
Columbia Theological Seminary

What Did the
Cross Accomplish?

What Did the Cross Accomplish?

A Conversation about the Atonement

N. T. WRIGHT,
SIMON GATHERCOLE,
AND
ROBERT B. STEWART

WESTMINSTER
JOHN KNOX PRESS
LOUISVILLE · KENTUCKY

First edition
Published by Westminster John Knox Press
Louisville, Kentucky

21 22 23 24 25 26 27 28 29 30—10 9 8 7 6 5 4 3 2 1

Unless otherwise indicated, Scripture quotations are from the New Revised Standard Version of the Bible, copyright © 1989 by the Division of Christian Education of the National Council of the Churches of Christ in the U.S.A., and are used by permission. In this book, Scripture may be paraphrased or summarized.

Book design by Drew Stevens
Cover design by Lisa Buckley Design
Cover art: Jesus on the Cross © Kathie Whitesel

Library of Congress Cataloging-in-Publication Data

Names: Wright, N. T. (Nicholas Thomas), author. | Gathercole, Simon J., author. | Stewart, Robert B., 1957- author.
Title: What did the cross accomplish? : a conversation about the atonement / N.T. Wright, Simon Gathercole, and Robert B. Stewart.
Description: First edition. | Louisville, Kentucky : Westminster John Knox Press, 2021. | Includes bibliographical references and index. | Summary: "N.T. Wright and Simon Gathercole discuss in clear and understandable language the meanings of the crucifixion of Jesus Christ. Their discussion explores various theories of atonement and looks closely at the Old Testament to discover Paul's meaning of his words that "Christ died for our sins in accordance with the Scriptures.""-- Provided by publisher.
Identifiers: LCCN 2020054573 (print) | LCCN 2020054574 (ebook) | ISBN 9780664265878 (library binding) | ISBN 9781646981892 (ebook)
Subjects: LCSH: Jesus Christ--Crucifixion. | Atonement.
Classification: LCC BT453 .W76 2021 (print) | LCC BT453 (ebook) | DDC 232.3--dc23
LC record available at https://lccn.loc.gov/2020054573
LC ebook record available at https://lccn.loc.gov/2020054574

For

Maggie,

Rosie,

and

Marilyn

Jesus' death launches, as a great act of cosmic and global revolution, the new world in which—with the grip of the powers broken—freedom, forgiveness, and new creation can flourish and abound, confronting all the power systems that still depend on idolatry and assuring the world of God's ultimate victory over death itself.

—N. T. Wright

What does it mean for the cross, meaning the death of Jesus for our sins, to take place "according to the Scriptures"? To touch on one part of the Old Testament framework, we see throughout the Old Testament that disobedience—whether that of Adam and Eve in the garden, or of Israel, or of the Gentiles—leads to death. The miracle of the gospel is that this link between our sin and our death has been broken. *Christ* died for *our* sins. Substitution is there at the heart of the gospel. Christ died so that we don't need to die. Christ bore our sins so that we don't need to bear them.

—Simon Gathercole

The earliest apostolic teaching on the atonement was performative rather than propositional. Simply put, Jesus' earliest disciples were engaging in atonement theology every time they took part in the Lord's Supper. Before any of the Gospels were begun, before any book of the New Testament was penned, even before Paul's Damascus-road experience, Christians regularly met and engaged in a ritual meal filled with atonement metaphors.

—Robert B. Stewart

Contents

Acknowledgments

Thanking others in print is always an occasion for anxiety because of the fear that some who deserve a word of appreciation will be overlooked through human error. But many deserve to be publicly thanked, and even praised, so we must go on. The dialogue that is featured in this book came from the fourteenth and final Greer-Heard Point-Counterpoint Forum. The Greer-Heard Forum was initially a five-year pilot project of New Orleans Baptist Theological Seminary (NOBTS) that began in 2005. The Forum was made possible by a generous gift from donors Bill and Carolyn Greer Heard, and was named in honor of their parents. The first Greer-Heard Forum was in March of 2005 and featured a dialogue between N. T. Wright and John Dominic Crossan on the resurrection of Jesus. It seems fitting that the final Greer-Heard Forum also featured N. T. Wright.

Apparently Bill and Carolyn were pleased with the results from the five-year trial period because in total there were fourteen Greer-Heard dialogues. So, first of all, we must thank Bill and Carolyn Heard for their passion to have a forum where leading scholars could dialogue about important issues in faith and culture in a collegial manner and on a balanced playing field. Without them, the Greer-Heard Point-Counterpoint Forum in Faith and Culture would be a dream rather than a reality.

The event would never have come off successfully without the efforts of Emily Sloan Jarrell and her staff at the Providence Learning Center of NOBTS. Vanee Daure and the media staff of NOBTS must also be thanked for recording it in both audio and video formats.

The initial transcription of the dialogue was done by Bryan Shuler. He deserves a word of thanks, not only for the transcription, but also for carrying out other tasks related to the project flawlessly and with enthusiasm. Lanie King Anderson must also be thanked for her assistance with numerous details related to the final Greer-Heard Forum. The late William Jackson III also was a great help in terms of logistics with the conference. In addition, Marissa Elias Wilson, David Gamble, and Micah Chung assisted in securing research materials for Robert Stewart. Micah also prepared the index.

Michael McClymond must be thanked for sharing an unpublished paper on the atonement with Robert Stewart, as well as Carl Mosser for several probing conversations with Robert Stewart related to the topic. Adam Harwood and Rhyne Putman read over a draft of Robert Stewart's chapter and gave encouraging and helpful feedback.

We very much appreciate Daniel Braden at Westminster John Knox for his interest in publishing this volume as well as his enthusiasm for fair-minded, respectful dialogue on important issues. Additionally, he was always timely in responding to questions and a source of much good advice and encouragement. Julie Tonini, Natalie Smith, and S. David Garber at Westminster John Knox must also be thanked for their assistance.

As always, our wives must be thanked; they are consistent sources of support. It is to them that we dedicate this book.

Theology, Worldview, and the Meal Celebrating the Cross

Theological Method and the Atonement

ROBERT B. STEWART

What is theology, and what is the role of the theologian? These are not easy questions to answer. Nevertheless, they are vitally important. Probably the answer most often given to the first question is "Theology is the study of God." This is, of course, the etymology of the word "theology," but understanding the constituent parts of the word does not tell us what theology is any more than understanding the constituent parts of the word "butterfly" helps us to understand those marvelous creatures.[1]

One answer found in a popular systematic theology textbook is this: "Systematic Theology is any study that answers the question 'What does the whole Bible teach us today?' about any given topic."[2] This is at best an incomplete, or perhaps myopic, view of the task of theology because the Bible tells us that God speaks to us not only through Scripture but also

---

1. The opening session of the fourteenth Greer-Heard Point-Counterpoint Forum included a dialogue on the atonement between N. T. Wright and Simon Gathercole, followed by questions and answers. The forum was held on November 10–11, 2017, at New Orleans Baptist Theological Seminary. The dialogue that follows this introduction is a transcription of that evening. As a courtesy to readers, some small editorial changes to grammar have been made to facilitate smoother reading.

2. Wayne Grudem, *Systematic Theology: An Introduction to Biblical Doctrine* (Grand Rapids: Zondervan Academic, 1994), 21.

in nature and history. If God speaks to us through nature as well as Scripture, then shouldn't theologians make the effort to listen to what nature has to say?

In this introduction I do not intend to give a once-for-all-time definition of theology, and I certainly don't have room for anything even approaching a comprehensive exposition on theological method. But I am persuaded that what theology is should, at least in part, determine how theology should be done. What one takes theology to be should factor significantly into how one goes about the task as a theologian. My goal for this introductory essay is thus more modest: I hope to identify something that is at the heart of theology and thus take a step toward doing theology well.

THEOLOGY AND WORLDVIEWS

Theology is an exercise in worldview thinking. Worldviews are fundamental to human life. They are like navels; everybody has one—even those who do not know what a worldview is. A worldview is a set of basic beliefs through which we interpret all of life. *Worldviews begin at a precognitive level*: they are argued *from*, not *to*. They are like eyeglasses through which we view the world, or computer operating systems upon which programs run.

Worldviews are inherently religious. Even if one does not believe in a traditional concept of God, one will believe in *something* that is ultimate. For instance, the term "atheism" depends upon the term "theism" to have any meaning at all. (Even the preferred term of many atheists today, "naturalism," is juxtaposed with "supernaturalism.") Because worldviews are inherently religious, they compete and conflict with each other. This is because *worldviews are comprehensive*; they make sense of all of life, or at least as much as they possibly can. Furthermore, *worldviews are also indicative*; they purport to tell the truth about the world and life. As a result, they are as much statements about what the world *is not like* as they are about how the world *is*.

Every worldview tells a story. Worldviews tell a story about each of us and life as a whole. Human beings are story-telling creatures. After serving as a pastor for over two decades, I never cease to be amazed at how quickly my sermon points are forgotten, yet how well stories about my family and personal experiences are remembered. Mark Turner states it well: "Story is a basic principle of mind. Most of our experience, our knowledge, and our thinking is organized as stories."[3] In other words, stories work on us psychologically in such a way that they inform and transform our thinking. Stories do this by presenting us with new ideas in a subtle fashion. Because they are not propositions or arguments, stories fly under our cognitive radar. They have the power to make new ideas normal. When a story is told often enough—not proved, not even argued for— it becomes embedded in our thoughts.

For example, I often ask my students, "If I said, 'I drove to class this morning at warp speed,' would you think that I hurried or that I took my time?" Invariably they correctly say that I hurried. I ask, "If I said, 'That man has the manners of a Klingon,' would you think that I was complimenting him?" They always answer, correctly, that I was not complimenting him. The reason they know what I mean is that we have a shared knowledge of *Star Trek*. The fact that *Star Trek* is a fictional story has no bearing on the power of *Star Trek* to influence our thinking.

Worldviews function as linguistic referees. They influence how we interpret not only reality, but also literature and history. This is particularly important where biblical interpretation is concerned. Consider Jesus' parable of the Good Samaritan. This parable is Jesus' response to the question, "Who is my neighbor?" (Luke 10:29). Luke tells his readers that the man's question was insincere; he was trying to justify himself, not gain information. My experience, over the years, has been that this parable is generally preached in American churches either as a moral story along the lines of what one would hear

3. Mark Turner, *The Literary Mind* (Oxford: Oxford University Press, 1996), v.

from Fred Rogers on his television show, *Mr. Rogers' Neighborhood*, or as an example of the dangers of legalism. It's not really either. Bear in mind that Jesus' audience was composed of first-century Jews. As such, they had certain worldview expectations about how the story would run and the plot moves it would make. To their ears, this was a shockingly subversive story. Jesus surprises them. Their expectation is that the priest and the Levite will help their fellow Jew. But neither one does. Then the Samaritan, whom they expect to be the villain of the story, does the right thing. Jesus' commandment, "Go and do the same," is not simply about how they should behave but also about whom they should not follow.

I tell the story this way to my students: "A new seminary student arrived in New Orleans early in the morning, before the sun was up. He got lost and ran out of gas. He left his car to get some gas. Unfortunately, he was robbed and beaten. A few hours later, a seminary professor passed by and, thinking that the man was drunk, said to himself, 'Some people never learn; the wages of sin is death.' A little later, a seminary student passed by and would have helped him, but the student was running late and had a test that morning. So he didn't stop but instead prayed for the man: 'Lord, please send someone to help him.' Finally, the atheist owner of a strip club on Bourbon Street stopped and helped him." Then I say to my students, "That feeling of revulsion that you felt when I said, 'atheist owner of a strip club on Bourbon Street,' is the same feeling Jesus' original audience felt when he said, 'Samaritan.'"

Worldviews provide a shared frame of reference for us. Worldviews matter because we have no chance of understanding Scripture if we have not entered into the worldview story that the biblical text presumes.

Worldview stories answer five questions:

1. Who am I?
2. Where am I?
3. What's wrong?

THEOLOGY, WORLDVIEW, AND THE CROSS 5

4. What's the solution?
5. What time is it (in the story the worldview is telling)?[4]

Note this well: a supposed worldview that does not answer these questions is not a worldview, however much one would protest to the contrary.

Christian theologians consider questions like these:

— Who is God, and what is God like (Theology proper)?
— How should I understand the natural world (creation)?
— Who am I (anthropology)?
— What's wrong with the world (hamartiology)?
— Who is Jesus (person of Christ)?
— What did Jesus do (work of Christ)?
— Who is the Holy Spirit, and what does he do (pneumatology)?
— What does it mean to know God / be saved (soteriology)?
— How should I live in my faith community and the world (ecclesiology)?
— When and how will God ultimately fix what's wrong in the world (eschatology)?

The task of the Christian theologian is to tell a story that weaves the answers to all these questions into a coherent whole. Theologians should tell a story about God and creation (where am I?), about humanity (who am I?), about sin (what's wrong with the world?), about Christ, salvation, the Spirit, and eschatology (what has God done, what is he doing, and what will he do to set the world right?), and do so in such a way that we can find our place, both historically and existentially, in God's story (what time is it?). When theology is done without a concern for the big story that worldviews express, the result is a collection of disconnected scenes of theological content, but the story as a whole is unresolved and, at best, only partially

---

4. The fifth question, "What time is it?" is not really a "what" question at all. It is a "where" question, but a where question that is asking for a chronological rather than a geographical location, that is asking, "Where in the flow of cosmic history am I?" rather than "Where in the world am I?"

satisfying. In fact, even when the pieces themselves are for the most part true, we are still left asking this question: "So what?" Meaning and purpose remain elusive apart from a worldview.

There is a symbolic aspect to worldviews. We communicate our most important beliefs through symbols. Symbols capture our shared experience in a form that communicates to those who know the stories at a glance. Symbols need not be visual, although frequently they are. Yet symbols must summarize the story, or key points in the story, and the answers to the questions raised in the story, or at its most important moments, making these key points and answers into a sign, a ritual, or a relevant expression. The ring on my left hand is a symbol that tells the world that I belong to my wife, Marilyn, and only to her, as long as we both are alive. It is not my marriage, but it reminds me, and informs anyone with eyes to see, that I am a married man living in a covenant relationship.

This should not be difficult for a culture in which everyone has a smart phone and understands how to use it. We don't read through a list of titles of digital applications to use our phones; we simply glance at a screen populated with icons—symbols—that picture what the function of the respective app is. On Facebook, we enjoy stories of significant events in the lives of our friends, such as births, weddings, graduations, promotions, and so on, by sifting through series of pictures—symbols that communicate the essence of these events in a glance.

Jesus gave his disciples two monumentally important symbols in the Lord's Supper and baptism—rituals that communicate the heart of the Christian story, that is, crucifixion and resurrection, in visual rather than verbal form. We shall return to the importance of worldview symbols in a bit.

Worldviews also function as ethical guides. There is also an inescapably ethical dimension to any worldview. Bryan Walsh and Richard Middleton state it thus: "A vision of life or any world view that does not actually lead a person or a people in a particular way of life is no world view at all."[5] This means that *worldviews are as much about ethics as they are about epistemology;*

5. Brian J. Walsh and J. Richard Middleton, *The Transforming Vision: Shaping a Christian World View* (Downers Grove, IL: IVP Academic, 1984), 32.

they are not only theoretical and conceptual. *Worldviews tell normative stories*: they don't simply give us an acceptable way to live; they also express to us the right way to live. In other words, worldviews have a performative and practical dimension; they are meant to be lived, not simply confessed.

Worldviews thus have a component of praxis. They are performed as much as they are professed. In other words, praxis—how one actually lives—is the truth serum of worldview analysis. Vance Havner put it well: "What you do today is what you really believe. Everything else is just religious talk."[6]

This means that when theology is done well, it will result not simply in new thoughts, but also in new lives. It not only tickles one's mind; it also transforms one's life. Theology done right produces a mission, not simply a thought experiment. Theology done well responds to the "So what?" question with a "Go and do likewise" answer. Theologians should thus reach their conclusions concerning any individual doctrine in a way that makes sense in and of the overall story. In other words, they should measure the part against the whole—and vice versa—in order to ensure that there is a fit between the two in such a way that one's life is redirected.

For this reason, reading *The New Testament and the People of God* the first time was a life-changing experience for me.[7] In it I saw clearly a model that joined theology to worldview, in which history and language were integrated, that demonstrated how theology and ethics fit together, and how creation, redemption, eschatology, and mission were part of one grand vision for life. And I realized that this was the case for all cultures and times. The more I have contemplated the task of theology, the more convinced I am that in his basic model, N. T. Wright is right. One may disagree with the content he puts into his model, one may reject his conclusions, or one may augment his model. But until one provides me with a more comprehensive model of how to do theology, a model that has more explanatory power

---

6. Vance Havner (1901–86) was an American evangelist. He often said this, or something like this, in sermons. I heard him on more than one occasion both before and after my conversion.

7. N. T. Wright, *Christian Origins and the Question of God*, vol. 1, *The New Testament and the People of God* (Minneapolis: Fortress Press, 1992), esp. 3–144.

and that more effectively translates theory into a mission for life, I remain convinced that, concerning the method and purpose of theology, Wright is basically right.

This means that when examining any doctrine, theologians should do their best to connect all the dots. Doctrines may be distinguished in theology textbooks, but they should not be divided. No individual doctrine stands apart from others. Conclusions drawn concerning one doctrine necessarily impact other doctrines. Consider the subject of this volume, the atonement. What one thinks of sin will influence one's understanding of salvation. What one thinks of God will determine how one thinks of humanity. And, of course, what one thinks of Christ's person will influence what one thinks of his work. I could go on.

Theologians take great risks when they ignore their own presuppositions. All theologians have worldviews, which are precognitive. We don't construct our worldviews; we simply have one. Worldviews can be critiqued and altered, but they cannot be avoided. Theologians like Athanasius, Anselm, Abelard, Luther, Calvin, Grotius, and Aulén all had their own presuppositions, which influenced how they understood the cross and how they communicated their beliefs. Recognition of the impact of worldviews and their resultant presuppositions is hugely significant when studying any doctrine, and especially so in the case of atonement.

Patristic theologians who advocated for the ransom and recapitulation theories of the atonement were significantly influenced by both the systematic persecution of Christians and the influence of dualistic metaphysics as seen in the various schools of gnostic thought that were seemingly everywhere in the earliest Christian centuries.[8] Anselm was influenced by the feudal system of his day and thus wrote in terms of honor and satisfaction.[9] Others, such as Luther and Calvin, were also

---

8. For a brief treatment of these topics and some useful bibliography for further research on this idea, see Ben Pugh, *Atonement Theories: A Way through the Maze* (Eugene, OR: Cascade Books, 2014), 1–25.

9. The degree to which Anselm was influenced by feudalism seems to have been overstated by systematic theologians who have surveyed the history of the doctrine of atonement. Nevertheless, it is undeniable that such influence was there.

products of their cultures—as are we today. I mention this not to criticize theologians past or present, but simply to stress that no theologian works in a vacuum; they responded to their culture as their culture worked on them—and so do we. In other words, none of us can get entirely outside our cultures. We may reject specific ideologies prevalent in our culture, but we will do so as creatures of our culture, using terms and means that our culture recognizes and to some degree produces. In other words, presuppositions are not simply things that other people have.

For this reason, theologians need to be as skeptical of their skepticism as they are of the beliefs of others. Theologians thus need to exercise a healthy hermeneutic of suspicion. There is a difference, however, between a healthy hermeneutic of suspicion and hermeneutical paranoia. Hermeneutical paranoia leads to thinking that all truth claims are nothing more than power plays or are indications of some subconscious need on the part of one purporting to know the truth on a matter. A healthy hermeneutic of suspicion recognizes that all human beings and societies desire power and thus seek to gain or maintain it when faced with differing perspectives. But a healthy hermeneutic does not, for that reason alone, conclude that a truth claim is automatically false simply because it is a truth claim. A healthy hermeneutic of suspicion asks questions like this: "What do you—or I—stand to gain by one interpretation rather than another?" and "Why should I believe you—or you believe me—on this matter?" It does not say, "Because you benefit in some way from your belief, your conclusion is therefore illegitimate." Someone may benefit from the truth; that has no bearing on the truth. For instance, I have invested a great deal of emotional energy in, and also stand to gain a great deal from, the belief that my wife loves me. Yet this is no unfounded or naive belief. I, and others, over thirty-six years, have found a great deal of evidence to support this belief. Suspicion and paranoia are not the same thing. Suspicion is being on guard for ulterior motivations and insisting on evidence before believing. Paranoia is believing a conclusion is tied to some ulterior motivation despite a lack of evidence to support that belief.

Suspicion is similar to skepticism, which insists on reasons for believing; paranoia more nearly resembles cynicism, which will not believe even when given a reason to do so.

The doctrine of the atonement is an ideal subject to test what I am advocating. The cross is, after all, the crux (no pun intended) of the matter for Christians. But doesn't the fact that the cross is the center of the Christian theology seem, if I may say so, a bit odd?

Does it not seem odd that when Paul came to Corinth, he was resolved not to preach the greatness of God, or the love of God, or even the law of God, but rather the crucifixion of Jesus, a messianic claimant who had been brutally killed like so many "messiahs" before him? Does it not seem odd that near the end of his First Letter to the Corinthians, Paul wrote, "For what I received I passed on to you *as of first importance*: that Christ died for our sins according to the Scriptures"?[10] What of the sort of death by which Jesus died? Crucifixion, one of the lowest forms of death in the ancient Greco-Roman world, was so low that Roman citizens were almost never crucified![11] Even though crucifixion was a notoriously inefficient form of execution, it nevertheless was a very effective form of intimidation. Not only did victims of crucifixion die a humiliating and excruciating death, they also were generally denied a proper burial.[12] In a culture where the majority of the religions had strict guidelines for what to do with a body after death, this was in effect a declaration: "You may choose your preferred deity, but remember this: Caesar is Lord!" Yet Jesus

---

10. This is 1 Cor. 15:3, emphasis added. Many have thought that this section is a creed or an ecclesial formula of the early church. If this is the case, then the oddness of the claim is heightened even more by the fact that the early church, from the first, proclaimed the death of their leader.

11. Cicero refers to a Roman citizen, one Publius Gavius, being crucified by Verres in *In Verrem* 2.5.63. The fact that this is mentioned in a speech by Cicero against Verres at the trial of Verres, indicates that it possibly was illegal. (Any conclusions drawn from this must be made with the awareness that Cicero was the consummate politician.) Thanks to Simon Gathercole for pointing me to this outlier.

12. For an informative essay on Jewish deaths being a somewhat frequent exception, see Craig A. Evans, "Getting the Burial Traditions and Evidences Right," in *How God Became Jesus: The Real Origins of Belief in Jesus' Divine Nature—A Response to Bart D. Ehrman*, ed. Michael F. Bird (Grand Rapids: Zondervan Academic, 2014), 71–93. It is not insignificant since, for Jews, crucifixion, or making someone die "on a tree," was enough to curse the victim (Deut. 21:22–23; Gal. 3:13).

turned this declaration on its head by dying on a cross and then rising from the dead, as if to say, "Is that the worst you can do?" As a result, his disciples boldly proclaimed that Jesus, not Caesar, is Lord! Does that not seem odd?

Does it not also seem odd that Jesus himself instructed his disciples to partake in a memorial meal that highlighted his death?[13] In fact, does it not seem odd that *the earliest apostolic teaching on the atonement was performative rather than propositional*. Simply put, Jesus' earliest disciples were engaging in atonement theology every time they took part in the Lord's Supper. Before any of the Gospels were begun, before any book of the New Testament was penned, even before Paul's Damascus-road experience, Christians regularly met and engaged in a ritual meal filled with atonement metaphors. Furthermore, if one takes the breaking of bread mentioned in Acts 2:42 and 46 to be references to the Lord's Supper, then Luke tied the presence and power of the Holy Spirit to the Eucharist equally as much as he connected the Spirit's power to apostolic teaching and conversions.

The Lord's Supper was thus practiced from the birth of the church. Furthermore, in 1 Corinthians 11:23, Paul stresses that he and Jesus taught the same thing concerning the meal, when he states: "I received from the Lord that which I also delivered to you. . . ."[14] Perhaps, then, the place to start in understanding the atonement is the Lord's Supper, the atonement symbol that Jesus gave us.

The earliest form of theology is not necessarily the most correct, authoritative, or complete—especially if one believes in progressive revelation. For example, if one believes, as I do, that the doctrine of the Trinity represents not an evolution (a change

---

13. Here I am not intending to argue for a Zwinglian "memorial" view of the Lord's Supper over against the Roman Catholic view of transubstantiation, the Lutheran view of consubstantiation, or the Reformed view of spiritual presence. I mean only that, whatever view one holds of the Lord's Supper itself, the meal is in memory of Jesus' crucifixion.

14. There is a disagreement over whether or not the words "I received from the Lord that which I also delivered to you" mean that Paul had some direct revelation concerning the Lord's Supper or whether he meant that Jesus taught Peter and others this, and then they instructed Paul. In either case, Jesus would be the authoritative source of the teaching.

from one thing into another) in Christian belief about God's being but rather the development, fuller understanding, and more complete expression of the truth that was always present in Scripture, then clearly one should not become non-Trinitarian simply because a Nicaean understanding of Father, Son, and Holy Spirit is not explicitly stated in the Gospels. On the other hand, one should not assume that the latest form of a teaching is the most complete, correct, or authoritative. Still, chronological priority does seem to matter when it concerns a universal Christian practice mandated by Jesus himself that represents the faith of the apostles.

The theology present in the Lord's Supper may have been the reason why the early church, to say nothing of the earliest church, apparently thought that the work of Christ was clear but that the person of Christ was mysterious! Council after council addressed the Son's nature and constitution, yet no ecumenical council dealt explicitly or primarily with Christ's work. Perhaps the reason the Fathers didn't address the work of Christ was not because they were clear on it but rather that there simply wasn't much controversy where it was concerned. "In Christ God was reconciling the world to himself" (2 Cor. 5:19), and that was all they thought they needed to know. They partook of the Eucharist regularly, and that was enough. Who knows?

One thing that we must be clear on is this: *the conciliar church is not the earliest church: the canonical church is.*[15] Historically speaking, Nicaea was further from Jesus than we today are from George Washington. One benefits from reading patristic theology, but the earliest *written* Christian theology is found on the pages of the New Testament. This means that the wrong way to teach about the atonement is to start with a survey of atonement theories. The study of atonement theories is useful, but

---

15. By canonical church I mean essentially the apostolic church. Some may object that the authors of the books of the New Testament came a generation or two later than the apostles, and thus the "canonical" church is not the earliest church. That is an important issue but also one that we don't have time for here. (I am of the opinion that the traditional authors were actually the Gospel authors.) Suffice it to say that the church we know through the NT documents is the earliest church to which we have access.

theories are not the best starting place.[16] In fact, the use of the term "theory" for the doctrine of the atonement is, historically speaking, a relatively recent phenomenon. To my knowledge, no pre-Enlightenment theologian ever spoke of his teaching on the cross as a "theory." Instead, they professed what they understood Scripture to teach concerning the significance of Jesus' death. There is a heuristic benefit to classifying theories of the atonement so long as one is conscious of the fact that theories are nothing but shorthand terms for ease of reference, not first-order theological statements. We should never make the mistake of thinking that arriving at the meaning of Christ's death is a simple matter of choosing between "theories," like choosing one flavor out of thirty-two flavors at an ice-cream shop.

There is also a difference between studying the history of a doctrine and studying the history that produced the doctrine, the context out of which the doctrine began. One approach seeks to understand a process, which is a "how" question: "*How* did theologians teach the doctrine of the atonement down through the years?" The other approach seeks to find an explanation, which is a "why" question: "*Why* did Jesus tell us to celebrate his death in this way?" Theories are thus not the place to start: Scripture is where to start![17] Scripture carries more authority than tradition. In fact, tradition has no intrinsic authority. This is not to deny that tradition is extremely important. Tradition informs our present theology and thus allows us to enter into a conversation with a larger, older, and more diverse community. Scholars should always be cautious when thinking that they have seen something that no other Christian has ever seen before. Theologians ignore tradition at their own peril. Ignoring *Scripture* on a subject places one at even greater risk.

---

16. The one exception is in the case of a systematic theology text that is limited in terms of space and therefore must intentionally survey doctrines rather than present them constructively (showing how they came to be).

17. Yet one *does* need to wrestle with critical questions as to context, cultural surroundings, and authorial intention—i.e., worldview issues—when studying the Bible. I am not here arguing for a simple biblicism.

ATONEMENT AND THE LORD'S SUPPER

So what does the Lord's Supper teach us about the atonement? At this point I cannot begin to do anything like a full examination of the Lord's Supper or the biblical passages that relate to it. My intention here is simply to point out very broad theological outlines that are obvious in certain specific New Testament texts addressing the Lord's Supper (1 Cor. 11:17–34, esp. 23–34; Matt. 26:26–29; Mark 14:22–25; Luke 22:14–23).

The first thing to notice is the great but not verbatim consistency between Paul's relating of Jesus' words and actions in mandating the ritual found in the Synoptic Gospels. There are differences, but the agreement is far more obvious than the differences. The idea and language of substitution is present in all of them, although in Luke it is most obviously communicated through Jesus' words concerning the bread, "This is my body, which is given for you" (22:19), and also in his words for the cup, "This cup that is poured out for you is the new covenant in my blood" (22:20).[18] The language of substitution is tied to the bread in the Corinthians passage, "This is my body, which is for you" (11:24); in Matthew and Mark it is voiced through Jesus' words concerning the wine. Still, it is there.

But more than substitution is present in the Lord's Supper. The concept of covenant mercy is also front and center. Sharing the cup shows recognition of the covenant (or new covenant).[19] The ritual is intended to remind believers of what Jesus did for them, yet also to remind them of how God has kept his promises and thus shown his covenant faithfulness.

The context in which Jesus inaugurated the meal was Passover. There is little doubt that he intended his disciples to

---

18. There is a significant textual issue in Luke 22:19–20. See Bruce M. Metzger's treatment in *A Textual Commentary on the Greek New Testament*, 2nd ed. (Stuttgart: United Bible Societies, 1994), 148–50. My point, however, is unaffected even if one brackets these verses in Luke as added after Luke himself wrote.

19. Here 1 Cor. 11:25 and Luke 22:20 read that the cup is the cup of the "new" covenant, whereas Matt. 26:28 and Mark 14:24 read simply, "This is my blood of the covenant." My position is that Matthew and Mark reflect what Jesus *said*, while 1 Corinthians and Luke reflect what Jesus *meant* by what he said. Regardless, the two are consistent, even if they have different wording; these differences are not contradictory.

understand that he was the sacrificial lamb whose blood would cover them from God's wrath and deliver them from bondage. There is no explicit statement of *penal* substitution in Israel's exodus from Egypt, but that does not mean that the idea is not present. The wrath of God was displayed against the Egyptians, but in the case of Israel, the lambs were offered so Israel would be spared (Exod. 11–12).

Fundamentally, however, the Lord's Supper, like the Passover, is about deliverance. The focus of the exodus story is on God's delivering Israel from bondage in Egypt because he is faithful to his covenant. God gave Israel a ritual meal to remind them of his faithfulness. Jesus gave his disciples a ritual meal to remind them of how his death delivered them from bondage to sin.

Deliverance, however, can come in multiple senses. A criminal pardoned from a legal penalty or judgment experiences forensic deliverance. Such a criminal is delivered from the consequences of unlawful actions. An addict experiences a different sort of deliverance from bondage. That bondage is not a consequence of a legal verdict; the addict is in bondage even if never arrested! Such deliverance is rather an internal change that affects the person's desires while going from a physical and emotional state of slavery to one of freedom. When delivered from the addiction, the former addict experiences not simply a change in status but also becomes a new person. Externally, sinners are forensically guilty; internally, they are spiritually broken and slaves to misdirected drives. Furthermore, there is also the bondage of a toxic environment. As I write, the world is facing the COVID-19 pandemic. We find ourselves in an environment of sickness and death. We self-isolate and practice social distancing in the hope that someday our environment will be more healthy. Sin not only condemns and corrupts our persons; it also infects and infests our cultures. Jesus' death truly liberates his disciples by delivering them from all three sorts of bondage (forensic, internal, environmental).

This results not only in release from prison but also in adoption. Believers become part of God's family, thus brothers and sisters to one another. Recognizing this, another word Christians have used for the Lord's Supper is *Communion*. This bonding is why Paul is so angry with the Corinthians for distorting the meal in a way that made the meal more like a country club brunch than Communion (1 Cor. 11:17–22).

The toxic environment is thus addressed; there is a note of eschatological victory in the Lord's Supper. The ritual not only looks to a past event—Jesus' death; it also points to a future event, his return, when the kingdom is fully established. The symbol [of the Lord's Supper] points in two directions rather than simply one; it reminds us not only of what God has done, but also of what God will yet do. Our future hope is grounded in what God has done in the past, in a way not unlike that of the Passover meal on which Jesus modeled the Lord's Supper. We have a hope that is based on the already-but-not-yet salvation that is thus grounded in history, here meaning the cross and resurrection of Jesus.

One thing that should be obvious and yet is frequently overlooked is that Jesus gave his followers a *new* meal. He reworked the Passover meal by placing himself and his death in the center of it. His death delivered from sin and death; his blood cleansed and made new. The promise that Israel clung to had finally been kept. God had delivered his people from bondage. The world was a fundamentally different place because of Jesus' death. The Lord's Supper is a celebration of that change and a reminder that a day is coming when things on earth are done as things are done in heaven (Matt. 6:10).

The Christian worldview symbol of the Lord's Supper, like all worldview symbols, comes with a praxis, a mandated lifestyle, a mission. The earliest Christians made disciples by declaring that, through Jesus' death and resurrection, God had fulfilled his promises to Israel. Even if some of those promises had yet to be fulfilled, they were no less certain because they were grounded in Jesus' resurrection. Furthermore, Jesus' disciples boldly proclaimed that Jesus, not Caesar, was Lord, showing that the cross is not only about individual salvation from condemnation but also about God setting this world right. Jesus' followers today must also resist cultures, powers, and leaders that raise themselves up into the place of honor that only God is due, recognizing all the while that there is a cost to do so. Those who do so will become people who bear crosses, not simply people who wear crosses. As we do so, however, the new creation is breaking through. The eschatological tone of the Lord's Supper reminds us that Christ's disciples may be persecuted, but they will never be victims! In Romans 8:31– 39, Paul declares that we are more than conquerors; he ties our inevitable victory to the death and resurrection of Jesus.

No one metaphor, model, or theory can adequately make sense of the cross. This is obviously the case: otherwise Jesus would not have given his followers a ritual that contained multiple metaphors for his work on the cross. Might one metaphor or model be dominant and the others flow from it? Perhaps. That question needs to be left for another day. The multiplicity of metaphors in the Lord's Supper requires that a full-orbed doctrine of the atonement will provide answers for how Christ's death has addressed the dual problems of *sins* (multiple individual misdeeds that render one guilty before God, and thus need to be forgiven by God) and *Sin* (cosmic, nonhuman forces, whether satanic or institutional, operating on humans and dominating humanity).

N. T. Wright and Simon Gathercole both allow for multiple metaphors of atonement in their respective works on the doctrine, albeit in different ways. We shall see how each scholar understands the atonement and how they interact with each other in the dialogue that is at the center of this book. Readers who pay close attention to each man's position will be richly rewarded.[20]

This essay is not an attempt at framing a complete doctrine of the atonement. Much more is required for even a sketch of such a thing, including a large number of texts from many places in the Old and New Testaments, as well as critically listening

---

20. Both men have written books on the atonement. See N. T. Wright, *The Day the Revolution Began: Reconsidering the Meaning of Jesus's Crucifixion* (San Francisco: HarperOne, 2016); Simon Gathercole, *Defending Substitution: An Essay on Atonement in Paul* (Grand Rapids: Baker Academic, 2015).

to and interacting with what others have said concerning the atonement in the past and what others are saying today. I have merely tried to give partial answers to the questions "What is theology?" and "What is the role of the theologian?" as well as tracing out a few of the themes concerning the atonement that we find in the Lord's Supper.

In closing, when we consider the cross of Jesus, we likely are faced with a mystery that is too great to be fully comprehended, yet it can be apprehended.[21] In reflecting on the cross, both the greatness and the goodness of God are revealed, so that we see both God's holiness and God's love. At the cross, God's glory and grace meet. At the end of our study, perhaps we still cannot entirely understand what God has done for us through the cross because of our human limitations. And maybe that's okay because God is greater than any human mind can fully comprehend. Why should we expect fully to comprehend God's work when we know that we cannot understand God fully?[22] Maybe we can know what we need to know even if we cannot plumb the depths of God's work. Still, I know this: when I partake of the Lord's Supper, the Eucharist, I am truly grateful. Perhaps the best response is not theology but rather doxology. Isaac Watts's classic hymn says best where our doctrine of the atonement should end.

> When I survey the wondrous cross
> on which the Prince of glory died,
> my richest gain I count but loss,
> and pour contempt on all my pride.
>
> Forbid it, Lord, that I should boast,
> save in the death of Christ my God;
> all the vain things that charm me most,
> I sacrifice them to his blood.

21. Comprehension is understanding a matter in detail as to why and how. Apprehension is simply understanding that a matter is true in some way. It is the difference between understanding how and understanding that.

22. Here I am affirming something consistent with Calvin's idea of divine condescension. John Calvin, *Institutes of the Christian Religion*, trans. Henry Beveridge (London: James Clarke, 1962), 1.13.1.

See, from his head, his hands, his feet,
sorrow and love flow mingled down;
did e'er such love and sorrow meet,
or thorns compose so rich a crown?

Were the whole realm of nature mine,
that were a present far too small;
love so amazing, so divine,
demands my soul, my life, my all.[23]

---

23. This hymn fits nicely with moral theories of the atonement like that of Peter Abelard. One significant difference is that Abelard posited that the reason Christ died was to provoke this sort of response, whereas Watts simply says that awe, humility, and devotion are proper responses to the cross, which I can't imagine many Christians denying.

The Meaning of the Atonement

N. T. Wright and Simon Gathercole
in Dialogue

N. T. WRIGHT: OPENING STATEMENT

N. T. Wright: Thank you for your welcome. It is very good to be back at a Greer-Heard Forum again. I do especially want to thank and congratulate Bob Stewart for his persistence and hard work in organizing these colloquia down the years and persuading all sorts of people to have, in public, the kind of conversation we all too rarely get to have in private. I am particularly grateful since my book *The Day the Revolution Began*[1] was published a year or so ago; I have been eager to take the discussion forward. This is a great way to do that.

In this opening presentation I want very briefly to put six major points on the table, one after the other. These are things in my book that I wish particularly to stress. (I should also say that there is an online course based on this book, which is among those offered at www.ntwrightonline.org.)

My *first point* is this: atonement isn't a "thing." It's a shorthand. We use the word "atonement" in Western theological

---

1. N. T. Wright, *The Day the Revolution Began: Reconsidering the Meaning of Jesus's Crucifixion* (San Francisco: HarperOne, 2016).

discussions as though there were one thing that we all know we're talking about, even though it is hard to say what exactly it is. The word "atonement" occurs in English Bibles at various points, but that is misleading, as word studies of technical terms will bear out. The term "atonement" is not well served by being seen as the name for a "thing," one specific truth. It is shorthand for a story.

All doctrines, you see, are portable stories. We fold the stories up, like clothes for a trip, and we pack them into a suitcase so we can carry them easily into and out of discussions. But the point of carrying a suitcase isn't because I like having a suitcase in my hotel room. (I wrote that sentence before this meeting, unaware that my suitcase was not going to be delivered by Delta Air Lines at the time of my arrival.) The point of having a suitcase is so that I can carry clothes, books, and personal items all together. The word "atonement" is a suitcase into which the longer biblical story is folded up. This is already done by Paul when he summarizes the gospel message in 1 Corinthians 15:3, beginning with "the Messiah died for our sins in accordance with the Scriptures." It would be difficult to have discussions in which we replace the single word "atonement" by that eleven-word statement, still less its completion with Jesus' burial and resurrection—just as it would be difficult to carry all my clothes, books, and other stuff onto the plane without the suitcase. So we pack it away, zip it up, call it "atonement"—then off we go into a hundred different discussions that are often more about the color and shape of the suitcase than about what is inside it.

This is not just a point about the way we use particular words. It is doubly serious. First, if we fail to pay attention to the story, if we never take the clothes out and unfold them and put them on, we are missing the point of the suitcase itself, never mind the clothes. We are, in fact, falsifying both it and them. Second, sometimes we may fail to pay attention to the Bible, or we simply use it to supply proof texts that, as the saying goes, "witness to a doctrine," to be slotted into a theological dictionary along with everyone else from Athanasius to Zwingli. If so, we are saying by strong implication that the

Bible is not really our supreme authority, but is simply a quarry from which we can dig stones to put up buildings of our own design. That is a serious charge for any theologian, particularly a Protestant theologian. When this conference took place, we were commemorating Martin Luther and the events of 1517. I know what Luther would say when faced with the choice of Bible or tradition. That is my first point: to remember that the word *atonement* can lead us away from the Bible and into much later tradition. We should always remember that atonement actually points in the other direction, back to the complex but vital narratives of Scripture itself.

My *second point* is this: The four Gospels are the primary witnesses, not just for the events of Jesus' life, but also for the meaning of his death. It is astonishing to see the extent to which the four Gospels have been marginalized in discussions of atonement. Generations of readers have found it hard, however much (as in my earlier illustration) they have folded them up, to fit them into the suitcase they have called "atonement." They have therefore salvaged only such small fragments as will fit into hand luggage, such as Mark 10:45, "The Son of Man came . . . to give his life a ransom for many." Gospel scholarship has followed and produced experimental methods and theories. There has been an implicit theological consensus that the Gospels are about Jesus' life, his teaching, and about the circumstances surrounding his death, but not primarily about the meaning of that awesome event. The Gospels may be, from one point of view (as people have said), "passion narratives with extended introductions"; but even those who have said that have not usually seen the theological point. Even my dear friend Richard Hays, in his wonderful recent book *Echoes of Scripture in the Gospels*,[2] focuses almost entirely on the question of who the writers of the four Gospels think Jesus was and is, rather than on the meaning of his death. (No blame attaches to that comment: the book was produced under extraordinary circumstances and is already long enough. But

2. Richard B. Hays, *Echoes of Scripture in the Gospels* (Waco, TX: Baylor University Press, 2016).

there is urgent need for a subsequent volume that would tease out what the evangelists, in their use of Scripture, were saying about the meaning of Jesus' death.)

Specifically, it has been fashionable in Gospel scholarship to downplay any possibility of Luke having an atonement theology. In part, this may be because he does not use Mark 10:45 when you might expect him to (at Luke 22:27). It is not always noticed that soon afterward Luke has Jesus quote directly—even more clearly than in Mark 10:45, in fact!—from the seminal Isaiah 53, and at Luke 22:37 we find Jesus quoting Isaiah 53:12, "He was reckoned with the lawless."[3]

There is in fact something else going on here, something a bit more sinister than simply a failure to notice scriptural quotations and their significance. Especially in the works of Bultmann's followers like Conzelmann and Käsemann, and those influenced by them, it became axiomatic that Luke had falsified the gospel by turning it into a historical narrative. This meant that he *couldn't* have held any "atonement theology," since in the presuppositions such scholars were working with, a "historicized" gospel stands over against the meaning of the cross. Here we see the same false antithesis between the gospel and history that has bedeviled recent discussions of so-called apocalyptic (see part II of my *Paul and His Recent Interpreters*).[4] This spurious antithesis of gospel and history has grown like Japanese knotweed over the last two generations, and it urgently needs to be dug out.

In fact, Luke—like the other three evangelists, but not like the so-called Gospel of Thomas and other similar documents—tells the story of Jesus as the focal point and climax of the story of Israel. It is in particular the climax of the story of Israel in exile, needing the good and sin-forgiving news of the kingdom, as in Isaiah 52–53. Still more specifically, Luke presents the story of Israel as the focal point of the story of humans and

---

3. My translation: see N. T. Wright, *The Kingdom New Testament: A Contemporary Translation of the New Testament* (New York: HarperOne, 2011).
4. N. T. Wright, *Paul and His Recent Interpreters: Some Contemporary Debates* (London: SPCK, 2013).

of the world. Ultimately, it is the story of Jesus' death as the climax and effective instrument of that kingdom-bringing, salvific mission. All four Gospels stress that Jesus chose Passover—not the Feast of Tabernacles, not Hanukkah, not even Yom Kippur—as the moment to do what had to be done. When Paul says that the Messiah died for our sins *kata tas graphas* ("in accordance with the Scriptures"; 1 Cor. 15:4), the word *kata*, "in accordance with," is every bit as important in this sentence as the *graphai* themselves. Far too much writing on what we have called "atonement" implies that Jesus died for our sins "in accordance with the scheme of Western modernity," to which we can append some "biblical" footnotes! That scheme is readily visible in hundreds of books, most recently and frustratingly in the new, huge *T&T Clark Companion to Atonement*,[5] for which one of the panelists in the present discussion has provided a complimentary "blurb." However many brilliant parts that volume contains, the whole is vitiated entirely at this point: in its failure to read the Gospels for what they are actually saying. So, that is my second point about the Gospels.

My *third point* is that the story the Gospels tell is a standing rebuke to our tendency to divide "atonement" up into different "models." Such an idea is wooden and disjointed, appearing almost deliberately to distract attention from what the Bible is actually saying. It is as though someone were to analyze Beethoven's Fifth Symphony by saying, "Well, in this piece Beethoven sometimes presents us with a dramatic rhythm; at other times he uses woodwinds to good effect; often he plays striking tunes on the strings," and so on. That might all be true; but the listener is still waiting to hear the music. The different supposed "models" all mean what they mean within the larger biblical narrative, which comes in five "moments." I shall briefly summarize these moments as follows.

The *first* moment is the claim that the long-promised exile-undoing new exodus has arrived. This brings, *second,*

---

5. Adam J. Johnson, ed., *T&T Clark Companion to Atonement*, Bloomsbury Companions 5 (London: Bloomsbury, 2017), 859 pages.

God's kingdom-establishing victory over the dark powers that had usurped his role. This is effected, *third*, through the representative, substitutionary death of Israel's Messiah, which dealt with the sin through which the powers had consolidated their grip over idolatrous humankind. Thus and only thus, *fourth*, the cross simultaneously provides the moral example of suffering love and also reveals, in a dark blaze of glory, who the Creator God really was, is, and will be. Thus, *fifth*, Jesus' death launches, as a great act of cosmic and global revolution, the new world in which—with the grip of the powers broken—freedom, forgiveness, and new creation can flourish and abound, confronting all the power systems that still depend on idolatry and assuring the world of God's ultimate victory over death itself.

Of course, all this depends upon a strong doctrine of creation, and also on the resurrection as following the cross and revealing it to be victory and not defeat, and also on the gift of the Spirit. As John (7:39) says starkly, this latter can only happen once Jesus has been "glorified," once he has revealed the love of God fully in his crucifixion.

We should specifically note that in this narrative, which fits together snugly and satisfyingly, the elements that are normally played off against one another actually depend on one another for their overall meaning. These elements, as is well known, include (1) the *Christus Victor* theme, which has often been played off against (2) "substitution"; (3) the notion of Jesus as the "representative," as "incorporating" his people, which again is often taken as an either/or with "substitution"; and (4) the notion of Jesus' death as a moral example, a sign communicating, "That's what love will do," which has been played off against all the above. Get the story right, however, and all these four models will fit.

It all depends, as I have argued more fully in the book, on the nature of idolatry and sin, with idolatry recognized as the root of sin. Paul's charge against the human race in Romans 1:18 concerns *asebeia*, "false worship," meaning idolatry; and then *adikia*, "injustice," meaning the fracturing of God's world and of human beings and their relationships. When we humans worship idols, we behave in subhuman ways, missing the mark of genuine humanness: "missing the mark" is *hamartia*, which we normally translate as "sin." That sin then constitutes the means by which the idols enslave us. Victory over the powers is thus achieved through sin being dealt with in substitution, which in turn depends on Jesus' representative messiahship.

All this is quite clear in the Gospels, once we learn to read what is there rather than coming with schemes of our own. It is particularly foregrounded in the narrative sequences leading to the cross, where Jesus' kingship is the major theme, highlighting the cross as paradoxical victory, climaxing in Jesus' dying the death that others deserved but he did not. We think, for instance, of Barabbas, or of the brigand next to Jesus. The Gospels thus offer us the narrative of *victorious kingdom inauguration through representative substitution.* This is, of course, substantially the story told by Isaiah 52 and 53, which itself draws into a single narrative the many other biblical stories of the great acts of redemption. The Gospels offer this as the focal point of the entire canonical witness to the meaning of Jesus' death and its role within the overall biblical story.

We may, if we like, call all this "atonement." But it is vital to remember that it is *this* complex story, rather than some other one, that is folded up within that beige-colored suitcase. That is my third point.

My *fourth point* is recognizing the language of sacrifice as part of the resultant story, *not* part of the story of "Jesus' bearing our punishment." I didn't talk much about this in *The Day the Revolution Began* because it would have doubled the length of the book, especially by including a discussion of the Letter to the Hebrews. What I need to say here again subdivides, this time into four subpoints.

The first subpoint states that the Levitical sacrificial system is not about animals being punished. Unlike pagan sacrifices, Israel's sacrificial animals were not killed on an altar, and the purpose of the blood ritual was to cleanse the sanctuary. The blood, the God-given sign of life, was the purgative agent through which all traces of death, including sin, which points in the direction of death, could be rinsed away so that the living God could do what he had promised: coming and dwelling among his people. How could he do that if the sanctuary was polluted because of their sin and impurity? Sacrifices then mean what they mean within the true, larger biblical story, which is not about how sinners can go to heaven, but (as Rev. 21 makes clear) about how the living God can dwell among humans.

The second subpoint about sacrifice is this. In early Christian thought we find the strange, otherwise unprecedented, early Christian combination of imagery from both Passover and the Day of Atonement. This is to be explained in terms of the exile. Unlike the slavery in Egypt, Israel's extended Babylonian exile was the result of idolatry and sin; accordingly, the victorious rescue (the new exodus) of the new Passover is accomplished through the great act of, yes, "atonement." But the point here is that through Jesus, as the resurrection and ascension insist, what is effected is not just the rescue of sinners from the consequences of sin (though it certainly is that as well), but the new reality of "Emmanuel, . . . God with us" (Matt. 1:23).

The third subpoint about sacrifice, therefore, is that the tradition developing during the long years from Anselm to the present, the last thousand years of Western theology, has made an illegitimate transfer of the language of temple and cult into the language of law court and punishment. This has had a massive effect on (for instance) our reading of the vital passage in Romans 3, as I have suggested in the book and in a more detailed article in the Festschrift for Richard Bauckham.[6] In Romans 3:23 Paul says that "all sinned and fell short of God's glory." But in the Bible, the divine glory is the glory revealed in the temple. Here Paul takes the same kind of charge leveled against Israel in Ezekiel 8:7–13 (as echoed in Rom. 1:23) and Psalm 106 and applies it to the whole human race. So, when the solution has been offered, Paul expresses the result precisely in cultic language: "We have been allowed to approach, by faith, into this grace in which we

6. N. T. Wright, "God Put Jesus Forth: Reflections on Romans 3:24–26," in *In the Fullness of Time: Essays on Christology, Creation, and Eschatology in Honor of Richard Bauckham*, ed. D. M. Gurtner, G. Macaskill, and J. T. Pennington (Grand Rapids: Wm. B. Eerdmans Publishing Co., 2016), 135–61.

stand, and we celebrate the hope of the glory of God" (Rom. 5:2). This points ahead to the conclusion of Romans 8, in which the whole creation becomes the new cosmic temple, set free from slavery to decay because the image has been restored and the divine glory, reflected in resurrected humans, dwells within it.

That is the larger context for understanding 3:24–26. Here I have changed my mind from all my previous expositions of this passage. Romans 3:24–26 is not speaking of the way in which sins are propitiated. The *hilastērion* is the lid of the ark, the place where the covenant God meets in grace with his people. And by our over-eagerness for some kind of post-Anselm or post-Calvin solution to the problem that we saw in Romans 1, we (and I include myself) have ignored the larger theme of God's dwelling with his people.

A telling sign of this new reading is in Romans 5:9. There the apostle refers back to the death of Jesus as the moment when we were reconciled to God through the death of his Son. But then Paul says that, as a result of being reconciled, we *shall* be saved from the coming wrath. If Romans 3:24–26 were somehow describing how that wrath was dealt with, Romans 5:9 would be a nonsensical tautology ("having been saved from the wrath, we shall be saved from the wrath"). This, of course, raises a thousand issues for which there is no space here.

As the fourth subpoint, we should reemphasize that Jesus chose Passover as the key moment for his kingdom-announcing work to reach its climax. The final meal that he celebrated with his followers, soon after his acted parable of judgment on the temple, was designed to begin his replacement of the temple function—the moment of intimacy when the living God deigns once more to dwell with his people—with what was about to happen to himself (cf. John 2:21–22).

This then leads to my *fifth main point*, which could be expanded into a whole monograph in itself but must here be stated with simple brevity. When Jesus wanted to explain to his followers what his forthcoming death would mean, he didn't give them a theory, he gave them a meal. The Last Supper, with all its sacrificial overtones (understood in the way I have just outlined), was Jesus' own final and definitive interpretation of the meaning of his death. This, of course, introduces an entirely new element into the discussion, moving us away from mental models and into the realm of the church's habitual praxis.

When we look back at the long history of "atonement theology," especially in the West, we find three things. First, we have Platonized our eschatology (with "souls going to heaven" in place of "resurrection within in a new heaven and a new earth"). Second, we have moralized our anthropology, suggesting that the crucial thing about humans is their keeping, or breaking, of a moral code, rather than their performance, or not, of their vocational tasks as the "royal priesthood." In the Bible, "sin" is the failure, the missing of the mark, in relation to that double vocation, not simply the performance of forbidden actions. Third, we have therefore paganized our soteriology. That is, we have taken the Pauline message of representative substitution through which the dark powers of sin and death are overcome, and we have turned that message into the idea of a vindictive deity lashing out at an innocent victim. All this is clearly spelled out in *The Day the Revolution Began*.

The distorted retrievals of Romans again provide the sharpest test case. We have assumed that the point of the argument is how to get to heaven, when for Paul it quite clearly is how God rescues and renews his creation. But the "getting to heaven" narrative, which is still massively popular and influential, is the teaching of middle Platonism, not the Bible. You will find it in Plutarch (e.g., in his treatise *On Exile*), not in Paul. Nor is this simply a matter of saying, "Oh well, let's adjust the destination; then everything else will stay the same." No! If you imagine you are a sinful soul needing to go to a holy heaven, your reading of the Bible, from Genesis onward, will be in terms of a moral scheme, in which—not to put too fine a point upon it—Western theology has put the knowledge of good and evil before the knowledge of God.

Look at it like this. Genesis 1, 2, and 3 do not describe God as assigning to humans a tough moral examination, which they then fail. They describe God as assigning humans a glorious vocation, which is self-servingly distorted. The answer to this problem cannot simply be "forgiveness." The answer must be "forgiveness and the renewal of the original vocation." That is how the original divine project of creation can get back on track. But if we insist, like Adam and Eve, on prioritizing morality (not, to say it again, that morality does not matter, simply that it is the necessary reflex of the vocation), then we will lurch toward pagan visions of how to get saved, pagan narratives in which an angry God demands an innocent victim so that his wrath may be assuaged, and so on. There is, of course, a biblical doctrine of divine wrath. But that doctrine is quite different from the all-too-common picture of capricious malevolence, which is what we find among pagan deities. Likewise, the Bible does speak of an innocent victim, but that is not the only thing to say about Jesus going to his death. Again, that death really does reconcile God and humans but not in the way ancient pagans imagined. Just as C. S. Lewis suggested that at the Last Supper, Jesus' words over the bread sounded as if he were playing the part of a corn king,[7] even though he'd never heard of corn kings, so the truth of Jesus' death appears to come perilously close to the pagan parodies. Perhaps we should rather say that the pagan parodies are powerful and seductive because they are so like the real thing, yet so fatally different. Although no self-respecting theologian or preacher would ever imply that God *needed* to kill someone, anyone, and it just happened to be his own Son, widespread testimony confirms that that is indeed what a great many, including young people, now assume that Christianity teaches. I do not believe in only teaching what people would like to hear. The scandal of the cross remains a scandal, but at least let us understand and preach the true scandal. As long as we persist in versions of the essentially pagan caricature, those who recognize it for what it is will either reject the whole story or they will do their best to find other approaches that play "Christus Victor" or "representation" or "moral example" or whatever off against substitution—or indeed, insisting on "substitution" and supposing that one must deny all other

---

7. In some ancient paganism, a "corn king" was a god, such as Adonis, Osiris, or Tammuz, who sacrificed himself for the sake of the land to ensure the next season's crop.

models in order to gain that point! Thereby they collapse the
biblical narrative once more into a low-grade smorgasbord of
"models," from which one then needs to pick and choose.

Finally, to conclude, the meaning of the cross is the revelation of the divine love in action. Nobody is likely to disagree
with that, but if you say this after offering the pagan soteriology,
the darkness attains a new bitterness. When an angry, powerful
person beats up someone else while saying, "I love you," this
is the stuff of nightmare, of sadism. Of course, what we need
is a robust Trinitarian theology, which is what the whole New
Testament and all the great theologians have struggled to give
us. God was in the Messiah and reconciling the world to himself. "The Son of God loved me and gave himself for me" (Gal.
2:20). Jesus, having come from God and going to God, loved
his own to the uttermost (see John 13:1). But this love is precisely the covenant love spoken of in Deuteronomy, Isaiah, and
the Psalms, the covenant love of God *for* Israel and *through* Israel
for all humans—and *through* humans for all creation. It means
what it means within that biblical, Genesis-to-Revelation story.

Speaking of stories, perhaps I should be allowed a concluding
one, which reveals the way that the cross powerfully leaps over
barriers of incomprehension and becomes, in itself, the strong
symbol of Christian apologetic. Cardinal Jean-Marie Lustiger,
a Jew by birth, was archbishop of Paris for the last quarter of
the twentieth century. He once told a story about three boys
in a provincial town who decided to play a trick on the local
priest. They went into the confessional one by one, and they
confessed to many weird and wonderful sins. The first two ran
away laughing, but the priest, knowing what was going on, set
the third one a penitence. "I want you," he said, "to go up to
that large statue of Jesus on the cross, and I want you to say,
'You did all that for me, and I don't give a damn.'" Off went the
boy. This was all part of the game. He said it once, "You did all
that for me, and I don't give a damn." Then he said it a second
time. Then he found . . . that he couldn't say it a third time. He
broke down and left the church a changed person. "And the reason I know that story," concluded the archbishop, "is that I was

that young man." The gospel message of the crucified Messiah, comments Paul, "is a scandal to Jews and folly to Gentiles, but to those who are called, Jews and Greeks alike, the Messiah— God's power and God's wisdom" (1 Cor 1:23–24).

SIMON GATHERCOLE: OPENING STATEMENT

Thanks very much, Tom, and thanks to all of you for coming and for the invitation. It is a great privilege to be here, and it is a privilege to speak on this wonderful subject of the atonement. I am going to focus on two points here, especially one, but two overall. What I want to argue is that front and center in the biblical picture of the cross, and the picture of the cross in the New Testament, are two points. *First* of all, the focus: God is reconciling people to himself. *Second*, the ultimate aim of God in reconciling people to himself: to bring glory to his name. Now I will come back to that ultimate aim at the end, but for the moment I am going to focus principally on this theme of God as reconciling people to himself.

Now, one of the concerns I have had in my research has been to show that a variety of different themes are in play in any properly biblical account of the atonement, to explain what God was achieving through the cross. It may seem a rather odd starting point, but I want to illustrate this from an Old Testament passage, Ezekiel 33–34, which I am just going to look at very briskly:

> If I say to wicked persons, you will surely die, but then they turn away from their sin and do what is just and right, if they give back what they took in pledge for a loan, return what they have stolen, follow the decrees that give life, and do no evil, then those persons will surely live. They will not die. None of the sins that they have committed will be remembered against them. (33:14–16)

> I will judge between one sheep and another. I will place over them one shepherd, my servant David, and he will

tend them. He will tend them and be their shepherd. I the LORD will be their God, and my servant David will be prince among them. I the LORD have spoken. I will make a covenant of peace with them and rid the land of savage beasts, so that they may live in the wilderness and sleep in the forests in safety. I will make them and the places surrounding my hill a blessing. I will send down showers in season. There will be showers of blessing. Trees will yield their fruit, and the ground will yield its crops. The people will be secure in their land. They will know that I am the LORD when I break the bars of their yoke and rescue them from the hands of those who enslave them. (34:22–27)

Why have I started with Ezekiel 33–34? These passages exemplify an important tendency in the Bible, a tendency that some modern scholars are not happy about. That is the fact that all the way through Scripture, we see two aspects of God's saving activity juxtaposed. On one side, we see liberation; on the other side, we see forgiveness of sins. In these passages, Ezekiel 33 records God's promise: "None of the sins that they have committed will be remembered against them." Then the next chapter (34) issues God's declaration: "I am the LORD when I break the bars of their yoke and rescue them from the hands of those who enslave them." Side by side we have the forgiveness of sins and liberation, breaking the enslaving bars.

The Ezekiel passage we just looked at also has an important third dimension to it. That is what we saw in chapter 34, that God has appointed a representative whom he will use to effect this salvation. In this third dimension, David is that representative. "The LORD will be their God, and [his] servant David will be their shepherd." God will save them, but David will tend the flock. This is not the historical David, who had been dead for several hundred years when Ezekiel was prophesying, but a future Davidic figure. Ezekiel was looking forward to that figure.

The last sentence of the book that I have written on the atonement[8] is from the Gospels and is quoted in the old

---

8. Simon J. Gathercole, *Defending Substitution: An Essay on Atonement in Paul* (Grand Rapids: Baker Academic, 2015).

marriage service in the Anglican Book of Common Prayer: "Therefore, what God hath joined together, let not man put asunder" (Mark 10:9). One of the concerns that I had was to argue that scholars who try to make one of these themes into the main theme make the mistake of thinking that what they have discovered is the most interesting fact in the atonement and that everything else is therefore secondary.

Some make representation the key theme. Some make liberation the key theme. Some make one specific aspect of the Old Testament the key that unlocks the meaning of the atonement. Several of these scholars, and those on whom I focus in the book, argue that there is a particular key theme in the atonement, which therefore means that substitution cannot really be one of the central aspects of the atonement. What I try to do in *Defending Substitution* is to show that substitution is actually an integral part of what is meant in the atonement in the New Testament. Attempts to say that it is philosophically dubious or that it is morally outrageous—the classic rhetoric about cosmic child abuse or whatever—is just so much useless rhetoric and simply demonstrates the presuppositions and prejudices of scholars rather than having anything particularly to do with the New Testament. Although for many, substitution seems like a natural part of the atonement, in the academic culture in which I live it is something regarded with a lot of suspicion. In fact, one senior scholar has even argued that Paul, in 1 Corinthians, is attacking substitution rather than propounding it. As I was writing this book, I remember talking to one specific scholar who asked me what I was up to. I explained that I was writing a book about substitution. This scholar replied, "Oh, Simon! Substitution! Even the word—ugh!" What had perhaps once been a sort of thought-out reaction against substitution had turned into a kind of visceral, emotional rejection of it.

Now in some ways this may partly be because there are some bad arguments for substitution out there. Tom has mentioned some of them. For example, the idea that the word *hilastērion* in Romans 3:25 refers to a substitutionary sacrifice is difficult to maintain. But as I say, in the climate in which I have been working, there is a great deal of suspicion about substitution, especially when it comes to understanding Paul's view of the cross. So what I try to do in the book is to take on what I regard as some of the most intellectually compelling alternatives to substitution, try to treat them fairly, but explain where they might have gone wrong.

In addition to the point that I mentioned earlier, many of these scholars take their favorite approach to the atonement and make that everything. One often finds another problem in scholarly treatments of the atonement. Some say that the focus of atonement, the focus of the cross, is that God, in Christ, is dealing with Sin with a capital *S*, the hostile powers, the forces of Sin and Death. Therefore by comparison, for God to be dealing with individual little transgressions is rather small beer, small fry. What is evident though, of course, in the New Testament is that a number of summary statements of what Jesus accomplished on the cross precisely describe Jesus as dying for sins, plural. I'll come back to that in a moment, when we will see that the forgiveness of sins and substitution are closely related to one another.

1 Corinthians 15

There are two passages that I want to mention briefly. The first one is 1 Corinthians 15, verses 3–4, and then verse 11 in particular: "For what I received, I passed on to you as of first importance, that Christ died for our sins according to the Scriptures, that he was buried, that he was raised on the third day according to the Scriptures. . . . Whether then it is I or they, this is what we preach, and this is what you believed" (15:3–4, 11).

Now I think this is worth a close look because here Paul claims that this is a summary of the good news. He says it is of first importance, not just a summary of what Paul, the maverick apostle, happens to preach. Paul maintains that it is a summary of the gospel that *all the apostles preach*, as in that last sentence.

There he declares that for all the resurrection witnesses, whether apostles or whoever: "This is what we preach, and this is what you have believed." So it is an important passage, an important starting point for what we think the good news might be.

What does it mean for the cross, meaning the death of Jesus for our sins, to take place "according to the Scriptures"? To touch on one part of the Old Testament framework, we see throughout the Old Testament that disobedience—whether that of Adam and Eve in the garden, or of Israel, or of the Gentiles—leads to death. This is made clear at the beginning in Genesis: "You must not eat from the tree of the knowledge of good and evil, for when you eat of it, you will surely die" [2:17]. Likewise, the curses of Deuteronomy declare, "The LORD will send on you curses, confusion, and rebuke in everything you put your hand to, until you are destroyed and come to sudden ruin, because of the evil you have done in forsaking him" [28:20]. Now that is what we might call the default pattern, if you bracket out God's grace. To take an individual example, there is King Zimri, not one of the best-known kings in the Old Testament, but someone whose end is described in language very similar to this formula in 1 Corinthians 15:3, "Christ died for our sins." The difference is that in almost identical language in the Greek version of the story, in the Old Testament, "King Zimri died for his own sins, which he had committed" [1 Kings 16:18–19]. That is the link between sin and death.

The miracle of the gospel is that this link between our sin and our death has been broken. *Christ* died for *our* sins. Substitution is there at the heart of the gospel. Christ died so that we don't need to die. Christ bore our sins so that we don't need to bear them.

Now then, since this link between our sin and our death has been broken, you might ask, "Doesn't that mean that Christ's death is precisely not in accordance with the Scriptures? If this is the case, is Christ's death in contradiction to the Scriptures?" Well, the Scriptures give the larger picture. In addition to this pattern of Adam and Eve and death, and Israel's sin and the curses of the covenant, there is grace, which in human terms is illogical. It doesn't fit the economics. In a sense it could even be regarded as unjust, in that God does not give us what we deserve. This pattern of grace appears throughout the Old Testament, in the sacrificial system in Leviticus, for example.

Yet where the rupture of this pattern comes supremely in the Old Testament is in the picture of the suffering servant, in Isaiah 53. In its setting in Isaiah 53, the figure of the servant has come into view as a particular individual. His contemporaries, other Israelites, persecute him to death and kill him. At the time, they regarded him as cursed by God, says 53:4. But at some later point, these Israelites come to the horrifying realization that what they had done rendered themselves guilty. It is what one scholar has called a "drama of delayed recognition." When the Israelites do a kind of theological autopsy or postmortem on this death, they discover that they were guilty and that he was innocent. Not only that, but this servant had, in some mysterious way, accomplished salvation for these Israelites. He had died both in consequence of their sins and in order to deal with those sins. This point is repeated over and over in the chapter:

> He bears our sins.
> He was wounded for our transgressions.
> He was beaten for our sins.
> By his beating we are healed.
> God handed him over for our sins.

And that is just a sprinkling of the many statements like this that we have in Isaiah 53.

One key point here is this constant alternation between the first-person plural and the third-person singular, to put it in grammatical terms: between the "we" or the "our" and "he." That's where the pattern in which we see Christ, "he," died for "our" sins comes from (cf. Isa. 53:10, 12; 1 Cor. 15:3). Here Paul is clearly tapping into substitutionary language, the substitutionary language of Isaiah 53, and so Christ's death is, in fact, in accordance with the Scriptures. But Christ's death is not confined to the original meaning of this passage, of course. Paul doesn't read Isaiah 53 as if he were a modern Old Testament scholar. He sees the suffering servant as a prefiguration of an even greater reality in Christ. Christ does not only die, as the suffering servant did, for his Israelite contemporaries. He dies for Jews, Israelites, across the centuries. And Jesus' death is for the sins of the Corinthian Christians as well. This is where we see the link between substitution and forgiveness, that Christ dying for sins means that the Corinthians don't have to and that we miraculously don't have to. This is an important passage; as I've mentioned already, it is "of first importance" (1 Cor. 15:3). It's introduced as a summary, in verse 1, as the gospel that Paul preached, and it is the instrument of salvation, as well as being the gospel preached by all the apostles. So I think this passage is a good place to start when one is thinking about the death of Christ as substitution in Paul's teachings, and then one can move on to other very similar passages like Romans 4:25, "He was delivered over for our transgressions," or Galatians 1:4, "He gave himself for our sins," passages with a very similar character to them.

Romans 5

In addition to this language of dying for sins, Paul and John and other New Testament writers also use the formula of Christ dying "for us," for people. Now this is a similar kind of formula, also used in Isaiah 53, but the expressions "Christ died for sins" and "Christ died for people" are slightly different. Romans 5 is a good entry point into what Paul means by this formula. This chapter sets the death of Jesus in its wider social environment, the pagan literary environment of Rome in Paul's day: "You see at just the right time, when we were still powerless, Christ died for the ungodly. Very rarely will anyone die for a righteous person, though for a good person someone might possibly dare to die, but God demonstrates his own love for us in this: while we were still sinners, Christ died for us" (Rom. 5:6–8).

In the middle of this passage, in verse 7, we have the general observation that Paul makes, with which pretty much anyone in the Roman environment would have agreed: "Very rarely will someone die for a righteous person, though for a good person someone might possibly dare to die." Paul is pointing out here that substitutionary death is a familiar idea, which anyone can understand. Substitution in general is, after all, an easy concept to grasp. Even a football player can understand what substitution is.

But substitutionary death, unlike substitutionary football, is rather rare. Orchestrating a substitutionary death, outside of a context of war, is quite difficult to do. Where people in Paul's environment might have come across this idea of dying in place of another is in literature. Not in the Old Testament so much; the suffering servant is one rare example out of the whole of the Old Testament. It is not really prominent in Jewish literature after the Old Testament either. But it is important in pagan literature. It is a fairly common theme in classical literature to find one person described as dying for another. And authors often use the same sort of phraseology as Paul does. The principal example in classical literature of one person dying for another has its roots in a play by Euripides from 438 BC called the *Alcestis*, and it has a special place in my heart because it was the first play I saw performed in Greek when I was a boy.

After the original play, the heroine Alcestis is referred to dozens of times in Greek literature, and she has a firm place in Greek mythology in the ancient world. Why is Alcestis famous? The reason Alcestis becomes famous is because she died in place of her husband. She is a model wife, a model heroine, offering herself in place of someone else. Greek literature is full of examples of one person dying in place of another, a spouse or a lover or a family member. Substitutionary deaths in the ancient world come in all kinds of literature: philosophy, history, drama, poetry.

Now Paul's point, of course, is not to say how much Christ's death is like this, but how much it is unlike it. Paul goes on, in Romans 5:8: "But God demonstrates his love for us in this: while we were still sinners, Christ died for us." The values that God displays in his love for us are completely at variance with what we see in the pagan world. The pagan attitude is illustrated quite nicely from this passage in Seneca, a first-century philosopher and contemporary of Paul writing in Rome: "If a man is a worthy one, I shall defend him even at the cost of my own blood, and play my part in the danger. If he is unworthy, and I shall be able to rescue him from robbers by raising an outcry, I shall not be slow to utter the cry that will save a human being" (Seneca, *On Benefits* 1.10.5). In other words, you need to calibrate carefully your attitude toward risking your life. Will it be a worthy object that you are going to rescue by giving up your life? Seneca says it must be a worthy person. You can shout, and call 999 or 911 to save an unworthy person, but don't risk your own neck. And this was a standard uncontroversial view.

Paul is very strongly contrasting God's love with this attitude. But at some level he is obviously comparing Christ's death with what it is like. You need to have some point of comparison to make a comparison at all. You can't really compare a hedgehog to Einstein's theory of relativity. You need to have some sort of grip in making a comparison, and the comparison here in Romans 5 is between different ways in which one person might die in place of another. Romans 5:6–8 is dealing with life-for-life exchange.

I have not hoped to cover everything on the atonement, but I've tried to focus on substitution. In a comprehensive account, one would need to explore all sorts of other aspects as well, the pastoral aspect, that substitution shows us God's love, shows us our sin, and gives us assurance of not having to die for that sin. One would need to integrate substitution with liberation and representation, as I mentioned earlier, as well as other scriptural frameworks.

The Purpose of Christ's Death

Above all though, I think, just to conclude, one would have to focus on the end of substitution, the end goal of Christ's death—namely God's glory. The cross is not primarily about us or about the world but ultimately about God's giving himself glory and glorifying his own name. "Christ became a servant of the circumcision on behalf of God's truth, so that the promises made to the patriarchs might be fulfilled and so that the nations would glorify God for his mercy" [Rom. 15:8].

POINT-COUNTERPOINT: DISCUSSION

Wright: There is a real danger here that we will just agree about things, so we will try to find some things where we actually have some point and counterpoint. But I guess since I spoke first, you should probably ask the first question, and we will just go from there.

Gathercole: Okay. How did Gentiles have their sins forgiven?

Wright: That is a great question. The more I was working on this book, the more I became aware of a really interesting point: for a Jew, the primary thing wrong with Gentiles is that they are idolaters. They worship idols, and the reason they sin is because they are worshiping idols. Therefore, the primary thing that needs to happen is that the power the idols have over them must be broken because when that happens, they can be welcomed into the people of God. And part of that welcome is precisely to insist that everything about your past is now *in* the past. It has no lasting effect in the present. That is the meaning of forgiveness.

Now, for me, the passage that expresses that best is John 12, where the Greeks want to see Jesus [12:21]. Jesus starts to speak about something completely different, it seems to us, but he ends up saying, "Now this world's ruler is going to be thrown out," so that "when I've been lifted up from the earth, I will draw all people to myself" (12:31–32). In other words, at the moment there is not much point in having a chat with the Greeks because they are just Gentiles. They won't get it. More important, the ruler of this world, the dark power, still has them in his grip. But Jesus then implies that, with his death, the dark power's grip is going to be broken.

When I started working on that theme, I realized that this is actually underneath the Letter to the Galatians as well. Part of the whole point (which you discuss very well in your book, if I may say so) comes in Galatians 1:4: the Messiah "gave himself for our sins, to deliver us from the present evil age." That is, the victory over the dark power, the saving victory over the dark power, the liberating victory over the dark power, that victory is achieved *through* the dying for sins. To put it the other way around: the "dying for sins"—which is for Israel and therefore for the world, with Israel representing the world—*breaks the grip of the enslaving powers.* That's the point of the Gentile mission. It isn't simply about going off to see if Paul and his friends can find some more people who need to know about Jesus (and who are too ill-educated to realize how crazy the message is!). The point is that the victory over the dark power has now been won. Paul can therefore go from Gentile city to Gentile city, knowing that the idols the people are worshiping are in fact a beaten rabble, knowing that any and all humans can abandon them with theological impunity (though they may face reprisals from angry or uncomprehending neighbors). Up until then, they could not leave them; but now the people can, because the idols' power has been broken. So that, I think, is the root of forgiveness for Gentiles. Does that make sense to you?

Gathercole: Well, let me think . . .

Wright: Please say yes!

Gathercole: I suppose that Christ's dying for our sins sounds like a funny way to express that. And I am not quite sure how you are saying that, on the one hand, the defeat of the powers is the means of forgiveness, yet also the other way around in Galatians 1:4.

Wright: No, no, no. It's the *same* way around in Galatians 1:4, because in that verse Paul says the Messiah died for our sins *in order to* free us, to deliver us, so it is the means of the deliverance. But this is one of the things I was going to ask you, about how you see what is going on in 1 Corinthians 15:1–11, which you rightly highlighted. I think this is very much underneath what Paul then says in 15:20–28, because saying in the first passage that "the Messiah died for our sins in accordance with the Scriptures" does seem to point ahead to the specifically "messianic" Scripture texts he cites in 15:20–28. But these messianic Scripture texts are, in fact, about the victory and enthronement of the Messiah. We find the influence of Psalm 110; there are repeated echoes of Psalm 8; we glimpse Psalm 2 in there and hear echoes of Daniel 7. I hope those tracking this conversation are all familiar with 1 Corinthians 15:20–28, where Paul insists that the Messiah has been raised from the dead as the firstfruits of those who fell asleep. There are multiple echoes of Genesis in particular: Paul is expounding the new creation, which refreshes the original project of creation itself. But then, in particular, he insists that the Messiah must reign until he has put all of his enemies under his feet (15:25–28); this is about the messianic *victory*, in accordance with the scriptural narrative. So I read this passage as belonging closely with the gospel formula at the start of the chapter. I suspect you do, too. But does that answer your question?

Gathercole: Yes, but the danger is just collapsing everything together and making it all the same. That's what I am wary of.

Wright: Hmm. No, I don't want to do that, because as I say, it is a sequential narrative.

Gathercole: Hmm. First Corinthians 15:1–11 is quite a distinct unit from what follows, since 15:12 sets a new argument in motion.

Wright: I don't like the idea of just these different models ("So Paul thinks of the law court . . . oh, and then he has the slave market, . . . then he does this and that . . ."). I think that is a way of disassembling the whole, and it needs to be reassembled in the proper scriptural pattern. But, yes, there certainly are passages that stress one point and passages that stress another. One more passage we should bring on board here would be 1 Corinthians 2:8, where Paul says, "None of the rulers of this age knew about this wisdom" because, if they had, "they would not have crucified the Lord of glory." He doesn't actually say that the cross was their defeat, but that is strongly implied. If Caesar and company, and the dark powers

THE MEANING OF THE ATONEMENT

that stand behind them, had realized that they were signing their own death warrant, they would have said, "No, no, let's not do that." Then, of course, there's Colossians 2:15, which speaks of the rulers and authorities being stripped of their armor and held up to public contempt. But the larger passage is, at least in part, all about forgiveness. Does that make sense?

Gathercole: Yes.

Wright: Good, good! Well, let me just ask you something, then, because you are talking about substitution, and I think I basically agree with most of what you are saying. I did especially like your argument about Alcestis, about somebody like that dying for a good person; and there are other examples of the same thing. I wanted to know about the times in pagan literature when people died for *bad* people—like Iphigenia dying so that the winds would blow in the right direction and the foolish king Agamemnon could have his expedition getting off to Troy after all. That was hardly a good cause: "We've got a war to fight; therefore, I am going to sacrifice my innocent daughter." This is not a good story. So, how does that work? Martin Hengel, in his book on the atonement, cites a lot of these things and then he simply says, "This is all preparation for the gospel."[9] I want to say, "Well, it was not like that." I suspect again that you probably agree more with me than with Hengel, but I would like to hear you spell that out.

Gathercole: I think one of the things I try to do in the introduction to my book is to disentangle some of these different ideas. So, for example, in some church circles we would regularly talk about substitution and propitiation as traditional Christian ways of talking about the atonement. Now, you can certainly have a system in which substitution and propitiation work together, but they are not the same thing. You can have a substitution that is not propitiatory, and you can have a propitiation that is not substitutionary. In the ancient world, a person might put up a monument as a propitiation to

---

9. Martin Hengel, *The Atonement: The Origins of the Doctrine in the New Testament* (London: SCM Press Ltd., 1981), 1–32, esp. 31–32.

the gods; that's a propitiation that is not a substitution in place of anything. Similarly, a substitution in football is not a propitiation. They are logically different things. Similarly with your Iphigenia example, where Agamemnon sacrifices his daughter because Hera has become angry with the Greeks and thus does not want them to sail to Troy and recapture Helen. That is a propitiation, but it is not substitutionary. And so, you might say that it is, in C. S. Lewis's terms, myth reflecting the gospel in some fragmented, refracted way, but it's not an exact analogy to the gospel.

Wright: But there are dangers. . . . Undoubtedly, I think we are probably both with Lewis on this: that in human culture as a whole, we notice all kinds of signs that God has not left himself without witness. The trouble is that if you then take one of those things and start from there and build your system out from there, then the whole thing is going to be distorted. That is one of the reasons why I was happy to know that Simon was going to be my dialogue partner here, because I think we are both committed to saying that whatever the tradition has done with these big "-ation" words, such as "propitiation" and "expiation," we ought to go back to the Bible and tease out some of the particular meanings underneath these rather modern technical terms used in translations of the original documents.

Can I then press you? When I read your book, I was waiting for you to turn over the page and get to Romans 8:3, because if I had to give one text that, I'm convinced, is a clear affirmation of penal substitution, it would be Romans 8:3. And I suspect that you, too, read it that way. So, since your book is on "substitution," I simply expected that this text might have crept in somewhere. Reading from Romans 8:1, the text says, "There is no condemnation for those in Christ Jesus, because" . . . "[on the cross] God *condemned sin in the flesh.*" Now that is definitely *penal*: Paul is speaking of "condemnation." And it is definitely *substitutionary.* Jesus dies, so therefore there is "no condemnation" for us. But we should note that he says, "God condemned *sin* in the flesh of the Messiah," not that God condemned *Jesus.* Now, are you happy with the way that works out?

Gathercole: There were lots of passages that I didn't discuss in the book, and I think in some ways Romans 8:3 is one of the most clear statements of penalty involved in the cross. I think there is something of it in Romans 3:21–26, but not via the traditional route of the word *hilastērion*, which both of us mentioned. To come to your formulation, I suppose it seems a little like a distinction without a difference to say that it is a punishment of sin in the *flesh* of Jesus, but not of Jesus.

Wright: Except that certain bits of the tradition have just emphasized that "God punished Jesus"; so I think it's quite important that the clearest statement we have on the subject very carefully does *not* say that. So this takes us back to your distinction between Sin and "sins": Paul says that God condemned Sin, capital *S*. I don't think that you have actually spelled out, so far this evening, what you think Sin in the singular really is and what it means when Paul uses it.

Gathercole: No, no, I didn't.

Wright: Well, could you do so again?

Gathercole: Yes. The main debate is over whether sin is a kind of internal tendency or post-fall flaw in the human condition, or whether it is a power out there, which needs to be defeated. I think it is very difficult to decide which Paul assumes. I suppose I tend slightly toward the fact that it's a sort of vacuous corruption. I take what in some circles is the traditional view, that evil is a sort of privation of being, rather than that evil is an entity with existence.

Wright: Yes, I am sort of agreeing with you about that. But as I was struggling with all the language in the New Testament about the defeat of the power of evil (whether you give evil a capital *E* or a small *e*), it did seem to me that there is something important going on here. After all, idolatry is a complex issue. In the nature of the case, if there is a good creation made by a good God, then evil, and everything to do with evil, is in the technical sense absurd. It doesn't make sense. That's why we don't really have good language for it, and I suspect the ancients knew that they didn't have good language for it either. It is shadowy; "evil" appears to be a power that is, as we say, "out there," but you can't quite get a hand on it. Anyone who looks back at the history of the last hundred years of the Western world would say, "There really does seem to be an evil that is more than the sum total of all the bad things that individuals do." But, to say it again, we don't seem to have good language for it.

So, how do we account for that? The account that I think the Bible encourages is to move toward saying something like this: When humans worship idols, we give to those idols a power over us that they wouldn't have by themselves. I see this in Colossians 1, where Paul says that all the powers in the world were made in and through and for Christ—but then, a sentence or so later, they are *reconciled* in and through and for Christ. However, in chapter 2, those powers are said to have been *defeated* by the death of Christ. So, it seems to me, we have to say something about how all that fits together, at least in Paul's mind. But in Romans 7, you have Sin, with a capital *S*; but the evidence for Sin (with a capital *S*) in Romans 7 is that "I" keep on finding that I do the wrong thing, that I sin, that I perform "sins." . . .

Gathercole: "Sin within me . . ." [Rom. 7:17–20].

Wright: Yes, "which is within me." But this interplay between "Sin" and the actual sins committed means, I think, that it cannot therefore be an either/or. I suspect that we may ultimately be agreed on that.

Gathercole: Yes, and obviously, as I'm sure you'd agree, the emphasis is on how evil is going to be overcome, has already been overcome and is going to be finally overcome, rather than on where it came from.

Wright: Of course, of course! That's right. The emphasis is always that there is a victory, which has [already] been won. And then, as in 1 Corinthians 15, the victory will finally be implemented when death itself is defeated and God will be all in all. And that's the aim, for God to be all in all; not for us to escape this world and go somewhere else.

Let me then take you off to deal with the *hilastērion*, the word Paul uses in Romans 3:25. That word has been variously translated, but one of its basic meanings is "the covering," the "lid" that sits over the ark of the covenant, in the tabernacle. The question of its varied use is complicated; it occurs elsewhere, for instance, in the stories of the martyrs, such as in the Maccabean literature. Take 2 Maccabees 7, a grisly story about seven brothers and their mother who are tortured to death for their refusal to abandon the Torah and eat pork. They are tortured by this Syrian megalomaniac king Antiochus Epiphanes. As they are dying, they are assuring the king that they will be back. They will be raised from the dead (7:9, 14, 36), while the king, when he's dead, will stay dead because God will punish him (7:14, 19, 35). But then, strikingly, they are saying, "We are suffering because of our own sins" (referring to the sins of Israel as a whole); but their hope is that through their suffering this will "bring to an end to the wrath of the Almighty that has justly fallen on our whole nation" (7:32, 38). The result is that in 2 Maccabees 8, suddenly, Judas Maccabeus starts winning victories. "The wrath of the Lord," says the writer, "had turned to mercy" (8:5). Therefore it looks as though the martyrs had drawn the sting of the divine wrath, the wrath that had taken the form of the cruel violence of the Syrian king. They had taken it onto themselves so that their fellow Jews might escape. The same story is told, with more of a philosophical twist, in 4 Maccabees (probably written around the turn of the eras), and at the crucial point that book declares, "Through the blood of those devout ones and their death as an atoning sacrifice [*hilastērion*], divine Providence preserved Israel that previously had been mistreated" (17:22). So I pose my question: Is that the same thing we then see played out in the New Testament, for instance, in Romans 3 [see 3:25]? And if so, where did the early Christians get that idea?

Gathercole: Well, I suppose I tend to see that as an idea similar to what you see in Isaiah 40, that in the punishment Israel has undergone, Israel has paid "double" for its sins (40:2). I don't think that means they have suffered double punishment, but they've probably received the mirror image of that.

Wright: The exact equivalent . . .

Gathercole: The exact equivalent, yes. Thus they've done their time, as it were, and so Israel now, having endured suffering, is ready to receive God's redemption. I suspect that's the same idea in 2 Maccabees. In 4 Maccabees, you do actually get the adjective *hilastērios*, which has that sense of propitiatory, but that's not the noun *hilastērion*.

Wright: So, what do you do with that? After all, this has been quite a hot topic in some American contexts recently, where some have argued, on the basis of the Maccabean parallel, that Romans 3 must refer to the *hilastērion* as a "propitiatory sacrifice." My first instinct was to think, "Oh yes, of course." But then the more I looked at it, the more I thought, "No, actually, I think 4 Maccabees is going down a pagan route, and that Paul is doing something quite different."

Gathercole: Yes, the adjective is formed from the noun, but I agree with you about what the *hilastērion* is. The ending *-tērion* means a "place," like a ceme-tery is a place where you *koimaomai*, where you go to sleep. And so the *hilastērion* is the place where God shows mercy; it's not the means by which it takes place. Can I ask you something?

Wright: Yes, sure, please.

Gathercole: It's really this stuff about vocation.

Wright: To be clear (British accents and all that), you mean *vocation*, not "vacation."

Gathercole: Your strong emphasis in the book, and the last point that you made this evening, was that the goal of forgiveness of sins is to get people back on track to reflect the image of God and be involved in the restoration of creation. I'm not sure that I've quite caught all the nuance there, but that's the basic idea, isn't it? So I think my concern with the emphasis there is whether what you are doing is to try to provide a sort of comprehensive framework for the atonement, and I'm worried a bit that the central focus of atonement *isn't* there, even if that is an indispensable consequence or peripheral component of the overall picture. So that when one finds what we regard as the sort of classic summary statements, whether it's something in Paul like 1 Corinthians 15:3–4 or something like John 3:16, "For God so loved the world [I'm sure you know it] that he gave his only Son, so that . . ."

Wright: Everybody in America knows John 3:16. I was once coming through customs and the customs man said, "So, what do you do?" I said, "I'm a bishop." He said, "You're a bishop, are you? What does John 3:16 say?" So . . .

Gathercole: Fortunately you knew the answer. . . .

Wright: I said, "Οὕτως γὰρ ἠγάπησεν ὁ θεὸς τὸν κόσμον, ὥστε τὸν. . . ." That surprised him.

[Gathercole and audience laugh.]

Gathercole: But a summary statement like that focuses on God's love in giving his Son, so that we might receive eternal life, not on the restoration of the cosmos and . . .

Wright: Are you sure?

Gathercole: Yes [laughs].

Wright: Because that partly depends on what eternal life in John means, and also particularly on how you contextualize John 3:16 between John 1 to John 21, which is the whole thing, which is about creation, new creation. But I would lay great stress on 1 Corinthians 15: part of the whole point of that chapter is the restoration of humans to be genuine humans—which is why the resurrection is so important to be genuine humans. And that in turn is nested within the divine plan to conquer death itself, so that—presumably in a now immortal creation—God will be "all in all" (15:28). But then I would say, Well, if you want summary statements of the cross, one of my favorites (and this is actually where I started the train of thought that led me into the *Revolution* book),[10] is Revelation 5. There, John the Seer sees the scroll of the divine purpose, which nobody can open. But one of the angels tells him not to weep, because "the Lion of the tribe of Judah" has won the victory. This is, of course, Jesus the Messiah, whose conquering death has qualified him to open the scroll, in other words, to take forward the saving and restoring purposes of

10. Wright, *Day the Revolution Began.*

the Creator. The purpose of this is clearly stated in Revelation 5:9–10, "You were slaughtered and with your own blood you purchased a people for God, from every tribe and tongue, from every people and nation, and made them a kingdom and priests to our God; and they will reign on the earth."

So here we have the purchase by the blood (the classic "atonement" idea) joined at once with the (perhaps unexpected) *purpose* of the purchase, which is that the ransomed ones will share the reign of the Messiah on the earth. The theme of "kings and priests" goes back to Exodus 19:6: this is Israel's vocation, and I take it (though I suppose this may be controversial) that this summary statement represents the human vocation to be image-bearers. Within *a* temple—and the whole creation is designed as the ultimate heaven-and-earth reality, in other words, as *the* true ultimate temple—the "image" is placed to be the means by which the rest of creation can worship the divinity (whatever sort of temple it is), and the means by which the presence and power of that divinity may be reflected out into the world. I think that's what image-bearing means. So there in the sharp summary statement in Revelation 5—liturgically and poetically formed, no doubt, but I think rather definite theologically—we find the statement of ultimate *vocation*, which is then reinforced later in Revelation too.

There is, of course, no one single statement in the New Testament that says absolutely everything about this. But if we are stacking things up, listing texts for consideration, then I would go specifically to Romans 8, where I see a massive Pauline retrieval simultaneously of Psalm 2 and Psalm 8. Paul sees those in whom the Spirit dwells as sharing the messianic suffering, victory, and glory. He is echoing Psalm 8, according to which humans are to be "crowned with glory and honor," with "all things put under their feet" (8:5–6)—one of the passages Paul is working with also in 1 Corinthians 15. Here is the human *vocation*, to be under God and over the world. This vocation belongs supremely to Jesus himself, through the qualification of his resurrection; yet his redeemed ones share this role: "shaped according to the model of the image of his

Son," as Paul puts it in Romans 8:29. So I don't see an either/
or in the New Testament between God's rescue of people from
their sin and its consequences—and his doing so in order to
reestablish and reaffirm their basic human image-bearing vocation. Of course, sometimes the one is emphasized and sometimes the other; but overall we need the whole reality.

Gathercole: I don't see an either/or, and I agree that we want
the whole thing. It's just where the focus lies, and I think you are
right that some of that stuff about the temple is controversial,
and the appointment of priests to God in Revelation 5 is quite
underdeveloped in terms of what it means.

Wright: And it's there in chapter 1. It's there in chapter 5.
It's there toward the end as well, in chapter 20 [cf. 1:6; 5:10;
20:6].

Gathercole: Yes, but in bullet-point form rather than
making it clear that this whole vocation is involved.

Wright: Yes. As so often in the book of Revelation (and I
am speaking as a fool on this, since there are experts here and I
am not one), I do think that the book consists of a massive and
gloriously complex retrieval of several Old Testament strands
simultaneously, and this human vocation is one such strand.
Yet it's clear that we humans can't be what we are meant to be
because of sins. When the power of Sin is broken (Babylon is
overthrown), its captives receive freedom from that power and
its results, which certainly means forgiveness. We are then free
to be who we are meant to be. Therefore part of the point here
is that, instead of the Platonic vision of just needing to get out
of this world and be relaxed souls sitting on clouds and playing
harps, we have the Christian vision of humans being made for
a purpose, a purpose that starts now. It isn't that, having been
saved, we then hang around and wait until we're allowed to
leave. We know there is work to do here and now.

Gathercole: Sure. I think there is a danger in caricaturing
the alternative when you start talking about sitting on clouds
and playing harps.

Wright: Well, I have heard it often enough in popular and
less popular circles, but still, be that as it may . . .

Gathercole: Yes, in the case of Romans 8, I agree with you about what the total consummation consists of; the work of redemption would not be complete without the restoration of the whole creation. But in terms of what the cross achieves, it seems to me that the created order, the nonhuman created order, is the *frame* to the picture rather than the picture itself, the stage on which the drama happens rather than the actual play.

Wright: Now that may be a point where we disagree. It seems to me that in Genesis 1 and Genesis 2, humans are simultaneously the crown of creation (however you want to put that) and the means by which God intends to work in the rest of the world. The rest of the world is not simply a backdrop for a drama that is essentially about humans. Humans are made to be caretakers of creation, priests of creation, and so on, because God loves the material world he made, and he wants humans to look after this creation of his. . . . I have a basically Trinitarian view of creation. I think God makes a world that is other than himself, with a creature in this world that is his own image-bearer, in order that he may appropriately come and be the true image himself. The *appropriateness* of Christology is there implicitly from the beginning; and we could say similar things about the Spirit, which will eventually flood the whole creation. But that's taking us too far afield for the moment.

Gathercole: No, that's important. But is the disobedience of Adam and Eve portrayed in Genesis, in the early chapters of Genesis, as a failure of vocation? Or is it just more straightforwardly a disobedience?

Wright: I think it is disobedience; the end of Genesis 2 and the beginning of Genesis 3 is still one of the most gloriously evocative and yet puzzling passages as to what exactly is going on. What does "the tree of the knowledge of good and evil" represent? And what is "the tree of life"? And specifically, if you are a Jew reading these things in the Second Temple period, how would you read that? What would you see as going on? In that time, I think you would see Genesis 1–3 as an advanced statement of the story of Israel: put into a wonderful land, given a task, rebelling, committing idolatry, being kicked out, and now wondering what's going to happen. The question of "priests and kings" is very vivid and important at that point; "priests and kings" is one way in which the idea of the "image" is retrieved in later reflection. Anyway, that again takes us too far afield. But certainly there are various emphases in different parts of the Bible; that doesn't mean they are contradictory or don't fit together. An obvious example would be Romans and Galatians. Galatians is written to warn people [Gentile believers] against becoming Jews, taking on the whole Torah, *in order to be* true members of the people of God. Romans is written to warn certain [Gentile] Christians who want to rid the church of Jews and Jewish life, Torah included. So Paul uses quite similar material for much of both arguments, but the thrust of the letters (as so often in theology!) is opposite. Does that make sense?

Gathercole: Going with you, what about Romans 9–11 and Israel in exile? Isn't Israel still in exile in Romans 9–11?

Wright: That is a really good question. The paradox of Israel in Romans 9–11 is one of the deepest and darkest places in the whole of New Testament theology. It is interesting how many other books raise questions whose answer is found somewhere in those chapters. A good example is Mark 4, the parable of the sower, when Jesus says that the purpose of parables is "so that they may look and look but never see; and hear and hear . . ." (4:11–12). So we think, "Wait a minute; aren't parables supposed to make things clearer, not to make things difficult?" And the answer is "Well, it's more complicated than that. Read Isaiah 6, which is being quoted, and you will find yourself in Romans 9–11 quite soon." The same is true in John's Gospel. What's going on with the Jewish people in John 7–9? To answer that, sooner or later you will turn to Romans 9–11. So what does Romans 9–11 mean? I think what Paul is saying here, among many other things, is that when you retell the story of Israel from a Jesus-shaped point of view, accepting that Jesus is Israel's Messiah (as in 9:5), then you see that the picture of the cross, the passion of the cross, is etched into Israel's own history. Paul declares that the cross is part of the strange but saving revelation of God to the world.

But at the end of Romans 10, even though the Messiah's cross has happened and the gospel message is now going out to all the world, he quotes Isaiah 65:1–2, "All day long I have stretched out my hands to a disobedient and contrary people." They are choosing not to look at, not to take advantage of, what God has already achieved. That, to me, is one of the key issues, which continues to be a major talking point in quite different circles, academic and popular. We need to press the question: Was Jesus really Israel's Messiah, or was he not Israel's Messiah? Because if Jesus really was Israel's Messiah, then every Jew in the first century would know that, if God really sent his Messiah, however surprising that Messiah would be, it would mean that Israel was being, as it were, regrouped, reorganized, and restructured around that person. Look at the Bar Kokhba revolt. To my astonishment, many Christians do not know about the Bar Kokhba revolt. One hundred years after Jesus, there was a man called Simon ben Koziba, who was hailed by Rabbi Akiba as "the son of the star," "Bar Kochba" [cf. Num. 24:17]. Rabbi Akiba and many other Jews believed that this character was the Messiah. Not everyone agreed. But they couldn't say, "Well, some of us think he is the Messiah, and some of us don't, so let's agree to differ." No. If he is the Messiah, then his movement and all that it means is the eschatological event: this is what God is doing once and for all, in and for Israel and the world. So people would either need to get on board or, if they didn't want to do that, would need to say that this man was a deceiver and leading Israel astray. And I think that same logic (with the difference that Jesus was a *crucified and risen* Messiah!) was driving Paul's retrieval of the Old Testament and, with that, his whole theology of salvation.

Gathercole: Shall we open it up for questions?

[Audience applauds.]

Questions and Answers

Question #1: Dr. Wright, would you please explain the difference between the covenant of vocation, that you talk about in the garden, and the covenant of works, and how you see that impacting what we think the aim of the atonement is? And Dr. Gathercole, I think if you have a point to make, that would probably be the best place to make it, as far as Tom Wright's argument goes.

Wright: Thank you. Great question! I am very much aware that I am in the presence of someone who knows a lot more about the covenant of works in seventeenth- and eighteenth-century theology than I ever will, namely, Michael Horton, who is going to be talking about this subject tomorrow. However, curiously, we had a seminar at Saint Andrews just last Tuesday, when my colleague Alan Torrance was talking about this very point. He was expounding (from his point of view, of course) the classic Post-Westminster Confession "covenant of works" as it is normally, I think, conceived. I wasn't putting words into his mouth! This is how it went. In the garden, God made a deal with the human race, a kind of moral covenant.

If they did certain things and didn't do certain other things, all would be well. That "all being well" might then be construed as "ultimate salvation" or "going to heaven" or "eternal life." Then, of course, the humans rebel. But that "covenant of works" remains in place—so *Jesus needs to fulfill it instead*. But before that, Israel is chosen. Israel is given the law, as a sort of second chance. And Israel does the same as Adam.

Now, at every stage of what I am saying, there are all sorts of footnotes that differentiate between different versions of this theory. I can't get into that. But the central feature remains: Adam and Eve were given a moral examination, which they failed, and Jesus then passed that moral examination on behalf of everybody else, simultaneously taking the punishment for the failure. I see that whole way of thinking as being ill-conceived at every stage. I just don't think that is what Genesis 1, 2, and 3 is about. I don't think that's what the New Testament is trying to answer. I think the category of *vocation*, what humans were called to do and failed to do, is particularly important. The human failure was first a failure of *worship*; that's the primary vocation. The failure of worship happens because people are worshiping idols; in the garden, Adam and Eve are listening to the voice of the serpent, who is challenging what God has said. And Paul retrieves that in Romans 1, "They worshiped and served the creature rather than the Creator." When you worship idols, you are giving power to those idols, and that power needs to be broken. Perhaps you simply say, "We did it wrong; therefore we deserve punishment—but it's our lucky day; someone else has taken the punishment." That might "work" at one level, but it is missing the really important point. And I do sometimes wonder whether the fact that the Western world as a whole is still so much in the obvious grip of idols, even the so-called Christian Western world, whether that condition might be because our theology for the last five hundred years hasn't named and shamed idolatry as the primary thing. Does that answer your question?

Stewart: And let me just say that if Tom has something to say about a question asked to Simon, do so. And Simon, if you have something to say about a question asked to Tom, feel free to do so as well.

Question #2: I was originally going to ask each of you what role, if any, the incarnation plays in the atonement, but Bishop Wright, at the end you mentioned your Trinitarian view of creation. When you talk about the Word coming to creation, you have a footnote in *Paul and the Faithfulness of God*[1] about "Incarnation Anyways" arguments. Do you believe, even without the fall, that the Word would have become incarnate?

Gathercole: I don't find those kind of thought experiments actually helpful, those sorts of "what ifs." Two important points, out of many that one could say about the incarnation and atonement, are relevant in our current context. A Trinitarian understanding, as Tom has mentioned, is absolutely vital to understanding the biblical statements about the atonement because it is not that God is inflicting punishment on a third party. It is God, in the person of his Son, dying. Second, the incarnation of the Son of God as a human being is also vital for a proper understanding of representation. The human race could not be represented by an angel or a saving dog of some kind: in such a case there could still be some kind of incarnation, I suppose, but an angel cannot represent the human race and die as a representative on behalf of the human race.

Wright: I just want to say yes. I am with Duns Scotus on this (though not necessarily for the same reasons). I think that God made the world in such a way that it would be appropriate for him to come and be the sovereign steward of the world in person, in the Person of his Second self, if you would like.

Question #3: My question is for Dr. Wright, but I hope that Dr. Gathercole will weigh in on it too. Dr. Wright, I'm not sure that you know, but your new perspective on Paul has gained some criticism over the past couple of years [everyone laughs] particularly . . .

---

1. N. T. Wright, *Christian Origins and the Question of God*, vol. 4, *Paul and the Faithfulness of God* (London: SPCK, 2013).

Wright: Yes, yes, well—I hear that the pope is a Catholic, too [everyone laughs].

Questioner: I think your work is brilliant. Last semester I had a chance to engage with a lot of it. One of the areas of criticism that I was hoping you might be able to speak to—because I engaged with some of your critics on it, but not you yourself— was the way that you handle *dikaiosynē theou* in 2 Corinthians 5:21, in particular. I am sure you probably remember how you handled it, and you may know what your critics said.

Wright: Yes, indeed. In 2 Corinthians 5:21, "God made Christ to be sin for us, who knew no sin, so that in him we might become the *dikaiosynē theou*," which is normally translated, "the righteousness of God." Everywhere else where the phrase *dikaiosynē theou* is mentioned by Paul—namely, in Romans 1:17; 3:21–26; and 10:3—it is strongly arguable that Paul is talking about God himself and God's own character and actions in faithfulness to the covenant. It is quite possible that 2 Corinthians 5:21 means something different. Paul is not absolutely tied always to meaning the same thing with the same phrase. But the strong primary assumption is that it might well be the same thing.

What sense would it make in that context if he were to say, "So that we might become God's covenant faithfulness"? Answer: Paul's argument from the end of 2 Corinthians 2 until the middle of 2 Corinthians 6 is "Look here, we apostles are ministers of the new covenant." And right after 2 Corinthians 5:21, he goes on in 6:1–2, where he quotes from Isaiah 49:8, "Now is the acceptable time, the time of salvation." That passage in Isaiah goes straight on to say, "I have given you as a covenant to the peoples." This fits perfectly with his line of thought from 2 Corinthians 5:18 to the end of chapter 5. First he says something about what God achieved through the Messiah; then he says something about what that means for his own ministry and calling, specifically his "ministry of reconciliation." The parallel of verse 21 with verses 18 and 19 then comes out most clearly if we read 5:21 like this: first, that God made Christ, who knew no sin, to be sin for us; second, so that in Christ we might be the embodiment of God's covenant faithfulness. That makes sense of the entire passage, back to chapter 3 and on into chapter 6, rather than simply being (as it's normally been taken) a detached statement of atonement theology. That is about as briefly as I can state it. I am simply summarizing what I said at the relevant point in *Paul and the Faithfulness of God* (881–84) and elsewhere. There will, I think, be some discussion on this tomorrow as well. Anything else, Simon, on that?

Gathercole: No.

Wright: Oh, he's happy with that. That's good.

Gathercole: Well, I didn't say that. [Laughter.]

Question #4: My question is primarily for Dr. Wright. You said, Dr. Wright, that our primary witness to the meaning of the atonement is found in the Gospels. You also explain how much of that meaning is rooted in the Jewish understanding of the exile. Am I accurate so far?

Wright: Um, yes.

Questioner: My question is how we would expect such a meaning to be found in the Gospels, when most of the Gospels are written to Gentile audiences. In other words, Mark is written to a Gentile audience, and Mark goes out of his way to explain Jewish customs and beliefs to his readers so his message can be more clear. Why didn't the Gospel authors, such as Mark, make their emphasis on the exile more clear?

Wright: Yes, thanks. That's a great question. I think the question of exile is deeply embedded in Jewish thought of the period. I and others have argued this way for a long time. There is now a book edited by James Scott in which I have a long essay expounding the point and several scholars respond to it.[2] This is not, in other words, a new point. So the question is this: How is this idea then freshly embedded in the early church?

One of the main things that went on in the early church was teaching. Most of Paul's converts were Gentiles. They

2. James M. Scott, ed., *Exile: A Conversation with N. T. Wright* (Downers Grove, IL: InterVarsity Academic, 2017).

didn't know the Old Testament stories, but Paul certainly wanted them to know those OT stories. Some of them would be functionally illiterate and would need to learn to read; but the main thing was to learn to read Scripture. Paul was teaching them, "innarrativizing" them (what a horrible word!), telling the story in such a way that it now *included them* in the narrative. That is a primary activity that was going on in the early church. Mark begins (in a possibly truncated opening) by referring to Malachi 3:1 and Isaiah 40:3, both of which are precisely referring to the end of the exile and in particular the return of Yahweh to Zion. That's what contextualizes the whole thing. Think of the very phrase "The time is fulfilled and the kingdom of God is at hand." You can't understand that unless you go back to Daniel 7 and Daniel 9. Those passages were being read by some in the first century within a way of reading the whole book. And in Daniel 9 we find the prophecy of "exile" lasting for 490 years, with all that follows from that. So Mark is actually soaked in this stuff. He presupposes it, and it emerges in many ways that might well have been as obvious to people then even as they appear opaque to most readers today because we are not thinking like first-century Jews.

So, on occasion Mark does indeed need to explain the details of Jewish customs (as, e.g., in Mark 7:3–4, with the "handwashing" question). But I think that everything in all four Gospels is dependent upon people being taught how to look at the world from a Jewish point of view. Where that doesn't happen, guess what happens in the next century: Marcionism. A rejection of Israel and the God of Israel. So, I think that a real challenge for the early church was to teach people to think Jewishly.

Gathercole: I think also there is a danger in thinking that the Gospels are like tracts and thus were just given out on the street. The Gospels would be supplemented with instruction by a teacher, rather than simply being freestanding entities.

Wright: Yes, yes, that's right.

Question #5: My question is for both of you. Tonight, you both have pointed to Romans 8 as a very important text for substitution, especially 8:3, and I agree with that. My question, though, is about what Paul does a few verses later, in 8:17, when he talks about the fact that if we are children, then heirs, heirs of God and fellow heirs with Christ, provided that we suffer with him, in order that we might be glorified with him. So, Simon, at one point, in passing, you said that Christ died so that we don't have to. But the reality is, of course, we *do* have to die and we *do* suffer. So why does Paul in 8:17 seem to make my "glorification with Christ" contingent upon my suffering with Christ? How would that fit into your theology of the atonement?

Gathercole: Thanks. I actually have a little section in the book, which you should obviously buy to get the answer to that question [everyone laughs], which is precisely a response to the objection that if Christ died in our place, then why do we still die? To answer that question, you need to look at the various types of death that Paul talks about. Paul usually refers to Christian death as a falling asleep. There are some exceptions to that, but they are notable exceptions. So, for example, where Paul does call the death of Christians a death is when someone is married to a spouse who dies: in that case, to somewhat soften the impact of death would be to lose the point or the fact that the person is free to remarry. So the usual language is of falling asleep. For unbelievers, Paul mostly uses a different verb, which is usually translated in English versions as something like "perish" (*apollymi* as opposed to *koimaomai*). So, there are different kinds of death in Paul's writings, and I think I isolate four different types of death, which helps get around the problem of the objection.

On the question of why we have to suffer in order to be glorified, I think that's because God's purpose is, as Paul puts it later in Romans 8, that we are "predestined to be conformed to the image of his Son" (8:29), so that involves, in our own lives, reenacting the life of the Son. I think you see graphic instances of that in the book of Acts, where first Peter and then Paul have their careers modeled on the way in which Jesus is portrayed in Luke's Gospel.

Wright: That is very helpful. I think particularly of the end of Acts, where in order for Paul to get to Rome, so that the gospel can be preached under Caesar's nose openly and unhindered, the penultimate chapter (which matches the crucifixion chapter in Luke) is the shipwreck, where the dark forces are doing their worst and they've all but got him, but he comes through it. And I think something is going on there that I suspect the church hasn't worked with enough. I know I haven't in my own thinking and preaching and so on. The point is that the victory already *won* through the cross of Christ needs to be *implemented* through the Spirit-enabled suffering of his followers. We find the same thing, only scrunched together, in Philippians 3, when Paul says, "That I may know him and the power of his resurrection, and the *koinōnia tōn pathematōn autou* [the fellowship of his sufferings], that I may be conformed to his death, that I may then share the resurrection of the dead" (3:10).

So I do want to stress two things. The inheritance is the new creation, and the "glorification" picks up the theme in Psalm 8, of the "glorification" of genuine humans being God's stewards in his new world. They will be the ones through whom God's will is going to be done in the world. The present form that this vocation takes—this is the third of my two points!—is the groaning in prayer that Paul describes in Romans 8:26–27, where, as he says, we don't know what to pray for as we ought, but the Spirit groans within us. I think we need to take that very closely together with Jesus' Abba-prayer in Gethsemane and his cry of dereliction on the cross.

Question #6: Dr. Gathercole, this question is primarily for you, but both of you could answer. Dr. Gathercole, you brought up two texts, Romans 5 and 1 Corinthians 15. You both talked about penal substitution. I was surprised that one passage didn't come up, which I always thought was one of the strongest on penal substitution: Galatians 3:10–13. In verse 13, Paul writes, "Christ redeemed us from the curse of the law by becoming a curse for us. For it is written, 'Cursed is everyone who hangs on a tree.'" I would appreciate it if you would address that in terms of penal substitution. Do you see that as a strong text? I always have. Why didn't that text come up in the discussion?

Gathercole: Yes, I do think it is a passage about penal substitution. Where I would qualify that, though, is probably something Tom would agree with—in fact, I know you would agree, Tom. For Paul, Gentiles are not under the law of Moses. This is a common understanding of Jews at the time: only Jews are under the law. Gentiles are outside of the law; you can see a clear statement about this by Paul in Romans 2:12: "Those who sin *anomōs* [without the law] perish without the law. Those who are within the law are judged according to the law." So the standards of judgment for Gentiles and Jews are subtly different in those two statements. Jews are judged in accordance with the terms of the law; Gentiles aren't. So when Paul says that Christ has redeemed us from the curse of the law by becoming a curse on our behalf, the "we" and the "us" there is specifically Paul and his fellow Jewish Christians, rather than being a universal statement about humanity as a whole being redeemed, being somehow under the law and under the curse. Therefore, the curse here is a summing up of Deuteronomy 24–28, where you have the curses of the covenant being brought upon Israel for disobedience.

Wright: Let's not forget Deuteronomy 32, which is one of Paul's favorite passages. Yes, I very much agree with that. The problem has come from Galatians being read as though it were the answer to the late medieval question "How do I get to heaven?" But that wasn't the problem that Paul was addressing in Galatians. Interestingly, Karl Barth in volume 4 of his *Church Dogmatics*[3]—written in the dark 1950s, some twenty years before anyone heard of a New Perspective—said the problem was that Luther read his own situation back into Galatians. So, this is not just some newfangled thing that Ed Sanders or I or somebody else has dreamed up. This is a shrewd observation by one of the great theologians of the twentieth century.

3. Karl Barth, *Church Dogmatics*, trans. and ed. G. W. Bromiley, ed. T. F. Torrance (Edinburgh: T&T Clark, 1976), IV/1:622–23; see my discussion in N. T. Wright, *Paul and His Recent Interpreters* (London: SPCK, 2015), 86–87.

Question #7: My question here isn't going to be about the Bible. I'm wondering if you could say a bit about the damned and how the atonement relates to them. Here's what got me wondering about this. In the sort of naive pop picture, we have this idea: God had to kill somebody, justice required it, and by killing Jesus, God gets to be just and send some of us up to heaven to play harps. On your picture, at least a large chunk of what is going on in the atonement is that we get our vocation back. But for the damned, that wouldn't seem to be the case. And not only would that not seem to be the case, not only would the atonement seem to fail for them, it also seems that the vocation we get back, that of being stewards and perhaps even cocreators, is something that looks like a section of creation cordoned off from the lives of the damned.

Wright: Thanks. I understand the question because it is a question that lots of people ask. It's not directly germane to what we were talking about. Nor do I discuss it in my book. (Simon, I don't think you discuss it in your book either, do you?) A very brief comment, then: I think that when God acts in the gospel, it is in order to recreate human beings, in order that they can be part of his purpose for creation. But God has made humans to be responsible image-bearers and will not undo that responsibility. And so, perhaps somebody says, "I want to go on worshiping idols. I really like *these* idols and *those* ones so much that I'm just going to go on doing that." What they are saying is "I do not want to be an image-bearing human being." The logical end of that road—as in parts of Romans 2, as in 2 Thessalonians, as in plenty of other passages we could look at—is what Paul calls "destruction" or "ultimate death" or something similar. What does that mean? You could see it, perhaps, in terms of someone just ceasing to be an image-bearing creature. They have made a responsible choice or, as you might say, an irresponsible use of their responsible choice. The problem comes—the problem of how we think about it, not the problem of sin and ultimate loss itself—if you stand back and try to make an almost mathematical scheme about "what God ought to have done." That is a problem with some systematic theologians, I fear (obviously nobody present here today), who start off with an apparently logical statement, such as, "If there were a sensible God, he would have done X. Now he seems to have done Y. Isn't that odd?" That is not how I am approaching it. I am trying to think, as it were, from Genesis forward and from Revelation backward. So that's where I come out: that image-bearing humans are capable of making an "irresponsible responsible" choice, to say, "I want to go on worshiping this idol, and I'm not going to give it up." We humans are capable of making that kind of choice. Simon, would you agree?

Gathercole: Yes, Romans 11:32 came to mind, where Paul states that God "has enclosed everyone in disobedience in order that he might have mercy on all." So, absent the cross, everyone is enclosed under judgment. And some people tragically choose to remain there.

Wright: Earlier in that chapter (11:23), Paul says, "If they do not remain in unbelief, God will graft them in again." That's "If."

Question #8: I'm interested in hearing opinions from both of you on this question. As we are having this discussion about substitution and the atonement, how would you relate this to Leviticus 16 and expiation?

Wright: To which? Sorry.

Questioner: To the scapegoat, to expiation.

Gathercole: Yes, I'll go for this.

Wright: It's your cue.

Gathercole: There are two different kinds of offering in Leviticus 16. There's the offering of the ram and one goat, which are both killed or slaughtered. And there's the other goat, which is offered live. And the scapegoat isn't really picked up in the New Testament as far as I know. It is developed by the fathers, but the New Testament does not really pick up on it. When Leviticus 16 comes in the New Testament, the dominant focus is on the bulls and goats that are slaughtered [cf. Heb. 10:3, 11].

Wright: But I think part of the point that we regularly miss is that the scapegoat is the only animal that has sins confessed over its head, which is precisely why it's not sacrificed, because it would then be impure, and you don't offer God something that is impure. You have just made it impure by confessing sins over it, so you drive it away. The main point of Leviticus, however, is not how sins get punished; it's how pollution gets cleansed. Thus at the end of the book of Exodus, you have (despite the sin of the people!) the setting up of the tabernacle. God then comes to dwell—not quite in the midst of the people, because he is actually outside the camp, just outside the gate: that is as close as he is going to come! He is there in his glory. That is the glorious climax of the book of Exodus in chapter 40. So therefore, Leviticus addresses the obvious question: How on earth are we going to maintain the dangerous presence of the living God right on our doorstep? The sins, the corruption, and the pollution of the people are constantly in danger of making the sanctuary uninhabitable for the divine glory. It therefore must be cleansed. Sins, and all other signs of death, are going to keep the Creator God at bay. So the sanctuary needs to be cleansed with the ultimate symbol of life, the blood. That's why, as I said before, the animals offered in sacrifice are not killed on an altar, like a pagan sacrifice. The killing is not the point. The blood, which is the life, is the thing that then cleanses the sanctuary.

Gathercole: I think, though, that when Leviticus 16 is picked up in the New Testament, say in Romans 3 or Romans 8, it is transfigured out of that tabernacle context, of course.

Wright: But because, as I said, one of the extraordinary things that happens in the New Testament is the unprecedented fusion of Passover imagery with the Levitical cult. Passover, and the sacrifice of the lamb, was never about the forgiveness of sins. The people were not enslaved in Egypt because they had sinned. God had come to rescue them. But the fusion of Passover imagery with atonement imagery—which before the New Testament only really happens, I think, in Isaiah 53— comes about because of the perception that the exile happened because of Israel's sins. The people in exile needed a new Passover because they needed a new exodus. But since the exile, unlike the slavery in Egypt, *had* come about because of Israel's sins, the new exodus needed to be both a rescue operation and a sin-forgiving operation. All this must be done so that Israel's God can come back at last to dwell with his people—exactly as in Isaiah 52.

Question #9: Thank you so much. Just a question for both of you two. We've broached on it. We've come close to it, but there's a word that, for the past several hours, has yet to enter any of this discussion thus far, and it rhymes with "bell." For a couple reasons I am interested in why we haven't used the word "hell" thus far. One text is Romans 8:3. If sin has been condemned, found wanting, judged, and so on, where then is the locus of God's justice displayed? The reason I ask this is because, a few years ago, Francis Spufford wrote this really otherwise interesting book called *Unapologetic*,[4] in which he declared that most modern, contemporary theologians had closed hell [and] had more or less said, "Hell doesn't exist. We don't need it anymore. It's an obsolete idea that has no relevance in the modern age." Now, of course, as we would all agree, that is a fairly brazen thing for one person to go ahead and decide. But I do pose the question: Regarding the atonement, what is the relevance of judgment to this vision of the atonement that you both are offering? Is hell obsolete?

Wright: The medieval vision of hell, which many modern, Western Christians still cling to, is indeed obsolete. It was always a retrieval of pre-Christian, pagan ideas of angry gods doing nasty things to people after death. That was an ancient pagan thing. (By the way, that was why Epicureanism happened, as a reaction against that. And you get exactly the same reaction from the 15th century onward with the retrieval of Epicureanism as a reaction against medieval theology.) So, the trouble is, as with the word "atonement" itself, the word "hell" means many different things in different contexts. Hence, if you just say, "Hell, yes or no?" I want to say, "I'm sorry. I refuse that. I need

---

4. Francis Spufford, *Unapologetic: Why, Despite Everything, Christianity Can Still Make Surprising Emotional Sense* (London: Faber & Faber, 2012).

to know what we mean by this." Many people are still thinking of a traditional Western doctrine. The Eastern Orthodox (I see we have some Orthodox colleagues in the front row!) don't do the last judgment the way that the West does. I was sitting in the Sistine Chapel once with an Archimandrite who looked at the great painting of the last judgment and said, "We just don't do it like that in the East," and I never got the chance to get him to explain how they *did* do it in the East. Perhaps Edith will tell us tomorrow. So there are various ways of dramatizing the notion of hell. We are not necessarily talking about the same thing. I am not a universalist, and I have never been. As I just said before, I think it is both possible and tragically true—I say tragically not least because I know people who are in danger of saying, "I am not going to worship the living God. I am going to worship idols. I find them much more congenial. They make me feel good about myself. Whatever." I think that is a way of saying, "I don't want to be genuinely human." And I think that sooner or later (I think C. S. Lewis put it like this), there are only two sorts of people: those who say to God, "Thy will be done," and those to whom God will sadly say, "Thy will be done." The loss of being a genuine image-bearing human, when you think about it, might seem far more scary than the scariest Dante-esque picture of hell you might imagine.

Gathercole: Paul pretty clearly said that Jesus rescues us from the coming wrath. That's how he puts it in 1 Thessalonians 1:10, that Christians are waiting for the Son, "who rescues us from the coming wrath." And similarly, in Romans 5:8–10, the atonement and justification are the basis on which believers can be confident that Jesus, the living Jesus, will save them from the wrath of God. That's clear.

Wright: So what about Francis Spufford? His book is interesting. It is well written. I disagree with many bits of it, though some parts are spot-on. I think he's hung out with a lot of modern, liberal, British theologians, and they represent a certain swath of opinion, but they are clearly by no means representative of the whole spectrum, even in Britain, certainly not in America.

Question #10: So, this question is for both of you. Dr. Wright, in your opening statement you brought up the importance of looking at the Gospel writers and their contribution to atonement theology. I would be interested to hear both of you elaborate on what that is, because for most of this evening we have mostly pivoted while talking about Paul. And I'd like to hear what you think, how the Gospel writers and the Gospels themselves contribute to our understanding of atonement theology, over and above conferring a description of how Jesus died.

Wright: Very briefly, it's about the kingdom of God. And people in the first century who spoke of the kingdom of God were retrieving, along with passages from the Psalms and Daniel, the famous passage in Isaiah 52:7–12, which is all about God coming back to be King. "Your God reigns!" is the cry. He is rescuing you from Babylon. The watchman will see him return. What will that look like? The prophet answers, astonishingly, with Isaiah 52:13–53:12. "Who would have believed," asks the prophet, "that *he* was the arm of YHWH?" The suffering servant is the one through whom Israel's returning God wins the victory, renews the covenant (Isa. 54), and restores creation (Isa. 55). So the Gospels indicate that all this was happening at last, through Jesus. At the same time there are all the echoes of Daniel 7, bringing with them also the promises from Daniel 2 (the "stone" that becomes a mountain and fills the earth, toppling the wicked kingdoms) and Daniel 9 (the "extended exile" followed by the strange messianic redemption). Daniel 7 itself is about the vindication of "one like a son of man" over against the monsters, the dark pagan powers. So the Gospels have a lot to tell us about God's victory over the forces of evil, and this is achieved through the suffering of the Servant. Once you see how Mark 1:15 works ("The time is fulfilled. The kingdom of God is at hand"), it means that all this is at last going to happen. We are then invited to read the rest of the Gospel through that lens, just like you read John's Gospel through the lens of the prologue. It will all fall out from there.

Gathercole: Yes, that is how it is in the Nazareth Manifesto, where the captives will be released and the poor will have good news preached to them, and as it is added in Matthew 11, the dead will be raised. These events show the kingdom at work, which will be complete in the new heavens and new earth coming already in the course of Jesus' ministry.

Wright: But it all depends on the victory that is to be won on the cross.

Question #11: This is primarily for Dr. Wright. You recently mentioned Alan Torrance. A lot of patristic writers, the Torrance clan, and some other people use a lot of language in terms of "redeeming human nature," so you get phrases like that and "the unassumed is the unhealed." You also hear that Jesus brought the divine nature to bear on humanity and raise it up, and all that type of stuff. I'm just wondering to what extent you think that is useful language for what happened in the atonement and if—to whatever that extent is, if at all—and how you might incorporate it into your wider model.

Wright: You are citing a lot of people there; and you quoted that line from Gregory of Nazianzus, "the unassumed is the unhealed," *aproslēmptos atherapeutos* in the original.[5] Yes, it was one of the cornerstones of the work of T. F. Torrance. That is important because it gets at the truth that God made his world in such a way as to be wisely ruled through human beings. One of the truths about God is that he is a working-through-human-beings kind of God. That is one of the main things that Genesis 1 and 2 are about. But if the humans are not doing their job, God is not going to say, "Oh, forget that bit. I'll just run it all myself then." God wants to rescue human beings so that they can resume their proper place within his glorious creation-restoring plan. That's how the whole story works. So then, the danger with some theories of the atonement (and I am not necessarily criticizing any of the people you mentioned) is that they think humans are just being redeemed *for their own*

---

5. Gregory Nazianzus, *Letter* 101.5, *To Cledonius the Priest.* Gregory knew that Jesus needed to be fully and completely human for God's soteriological purposes to be fulfilled.

sakes. No! The answer is that they are being redeemed because God loves them—yes, of course!—but also in order that, *in* his love, he will work *through* them gloriously and make them fulfilled as true humans in working for his creation project. So the theme of the restoration of humans, and (what you might call) the necessary humanization of God in the incarnation in order to accomplish that, is absolutely basic. If we find that difficult to understand, it may be that we have so structured other thoughts that we haven't left room for true humans. But if we go back and do it more biblically, then I think we will have to make room for them.

Question #12: This question is for both of you. Biblically, is the highest importance of the atonement to restore us to an unfallen state, as you would say, Mr. Wright, genuinely human, *or* is it to be vessels of mercy to glorify God forever?

Gathercole: Talk about an either/or! [Everyone laughs.]

Wright: The answer has to be yes.

Gathercole: I don't think it is just to make us into an unfallen state, as if all the cross does is turn the clock back to a prelapsarian Genesis 1 and 2. There is certainly a movement forward, so that Revelation 21–22 exceed the situation in Genesis 1–2, rather than simply repristinating it. But I think—this is probably an area where we are still going to get stuck and disagree—that nevertheless the focus of atonement is on us being remade as creatures who glorify God and praise him, and that secondarily, even tertiarily, we are part of God's restoring plan for the cosmos.

Wright: As I read Revelation 4 and 5, which form one of the most glorious pairs of chapters in the whole of Scripture, I see the whole creation praising God and the humans adding the word "because": "You are worthy *because* you created all things," and then "You are worthy *because* you ransomed and redeemed," and so on. One of the problems with theology is that you have to say everything all the time; otherwise people think that you deliberately left something out. You are absolutely right: everything is for the glory of God. Of course it is. That must be the ultimate thing. You cannot pray the psalms every day, as I have done for years and years, without constantly being brought into that place. At the end of his talk, Simon quoted some of Romans 15:7–13, which is a careful combination of passages from the Torah, the Writings, and the Prophets, all of which, as a whole, say that God is bringing the human race together so that they can together praise him. This is both the restoration of God's model for humans, specifically and precisely because the humans are to be the priests of creation, that they might glorify God. That is where the either/or just doesn't exist.

Question #13: I started as a student of history, and now I am a student of theology. When I study pagan mythologies, my understanding has been that although these pagans did believe that the gods demanded punishment during life, they didn't have an eschatology in which this punishment necessarily continued after death, except in extreme cases of acting against the gods. So whenever you say that [some Christians are] borrowing from a pagan understanding, from an eschatology of the gods as punishing people after death, I am personally not seeing where you are drawing that from. So I ask, Am I mistaken in this? Or is there another source from which you are drawing this understanding of eschatology?

Wright: That is a great question. Thank you. I am glad that came up because I think you see it best in the mirror, as it were. The philosophers are reacting against what they assume is the popular pagan belief, so that in Epicurus and then in his major statement by Lucretius (first century BC: a major statement of Epicureanism), they are waging war against a belief that must have been common since there is no reason why they would just have imagined it. Yet the sources for what they were attacking were not written up in the same poetic form, so we don't find strong literary evidence for those beliefs (except in older traditions like Homer and the Greek tragedies). On the other hand, in some of those Greek plays, you have the Furies chasing people and all sorts of similar things, horrors that might well pursue people beyond the grave. Part of the danger there is that the philosophers are philosophers, at least in part, precisely because they are fed up with ordinary, popular paganism, and they say, "It must be different. The gods, if there are gods, must be different from that." So then we need to look in that mirror and see what it is they are reacting against.

Gathercole: I think there is quite a lot of variety, though.

Wright: Oh, of course.

Gathercole: In the Platonic tradition there is quite a strong emphasis on the postmortem state. I think modern Western culture has divinized Plato as a sort of supreme rationalist, but he is not particularly a rationalist. He employs reason, Socrates employs reason; but when reason falls short, in comes the myth. And one of those myths includes the souls of the dead going into the Acherusian Lake for punishment. The Epicureans are at the other end of the spectrum. The Stoics are a bit ambiguous about life after death; there is some variety among the Stoics.

Wright: Yes, but yes, you are right. I had forgotten that bit about Plato. So there is evidence for it, but I think the evidence suggests a more widespread belief than there is actual written evidence for, and you probably see it on ancient tombstones, the sort of anxious prayers, because you can find some ancient tombstones that say, "*Non fui, fui, non sum, non curo*. I was not. I was. I am not. I don't care." It's a shrug of the shoulders: life's like that, death's like that, I don't care. But there are others tombstones that are actually expressing the hope to be delivered from something. There is a sort of half-named fear of something beyond. There we are.

Day 2: Concluding Comments, Q and A

Wright: Thanks. How does one reflect on a slice of living theology, as it were? I've jotted down six things that I just name. You've probably done the same.

Gathercole: Yes.

Wright: For me, one of the most interesting things is the discussion about exegesis and theology and how they go together. After all, you can't go three paces in exegesis without raising theological questions, and you shouldn't go three paces in theology without saying, "Wait a minute. How is this coming out of the Bible?" But we have not characteristically been good about doing that interface, or even thinking wisely about how that interface works. I think we have seen a bit of that today, and it would be lovely to think that this conversation has not only helped us think about the cross, which hopefully it has, but also helped us to think about the larger issue of how that works. I suspect you'd agree with that.

Gathercole: Yes, absolutely. I've been lucky in that I've worked in institutions where systematicians have been interested in the Bible. I was a colleague of John Webster in Aberdeen, and now

I am alongside Ian McFarland in Cambridge. So yes, this is something that needs to happen a lot more.

Wright: Yes. We are so busy in our respective silos that it's very easy to go on, year after year, vaguely hearing about what is going on in the other worlds. There isn't time to integrate. But it really, really needs to be done. Otherwise we are miles apart from each other. One of the things that has been interesting to me, of course—because I have been one of the people that has pushed on it rather hard over the last ten to fifteen years—is having others call us to account regarding how we think about ultimate salvation. Instead of imagining a soul going to heaven when the person dies, which is Plutarch's conception, we are thinking about new heavens and new earth, and about the integration of heaven and earth in Christ, which actually then does affect everything. And again, I know you agree with this.

Gathercole: Well, I think I partly agree.

Wright: Of course, you do agree, Simon. Let's be clear about this. [Audience laughs.]

Gathercole: Obviously it's not just a matter of tweaking things slightly when you introduce the resurrection. But I think, on the other hand, there is a danger that the alternatives are *either* the "works-contract" and the soul going to heaven when you die, *or* the full vocation and new heavens and new earth. There are quite a few options in between there.

Wright: You are adding more into that equation. I was meaning simply in terms of the ultimate eschatology: how do we talk about that?

Gathercole: Yes, I'm totally with you on the new heavens and new earth.

Wright: But then, I think it is a real growth point, and asking the question of the meaning of the cross raises this issue for me, regarding what we call "temple theology" and how we reconceive sacrifice, image, and many other central terms in terms of that temple theology. And then (we haven't said this in the present discussion, but) when Jesus came to Jerusalem, knowing what he had to do, the principal thing he did was the demonstration in the temple. On that, I stand with those who say that what Jesus did in the temple and what he did in the upper room (Mark 14:15 and par.) were mutually explanatory, in terms of the announcement that the present system was under God's judgment. This then points forward to the Last Supper—which is somehow instituting something that will take the temple's place, with Jesus himself, not a building, as the focus. I suspect you agree with that, but we haven't actually talked about that during this last twenty-four hours. Yet I think this is Jesus' own interpretation of the meaning of his death.

Gathercole: Yes, I think the temple is important, but I wouldn't go as far with it as you do in this. I think, for example, sometimes you emphasize strongly that glorification is a temple image. I'm not so convinced about that. Obviously, the temple is one context of glory. As you point out, Psalm 8 is another. There are various contexts in which glory and image language sit in the Old Testament.

Wright: But if you are a Jew of the Second Temple period, and somebody says something about the restoration of the glory of God, the natural way of reading that would be the end of the book of Ezekiel, which is a reprise of the end of Exodus, that there will be a new temple and finally the glory will come back and live there. Then, in Luke, we have people saying, "God has visited his people," which obviously is a Lukan theme; and then, particularly, Jesus saying the temple is going to be destroyed, and so on, because "you didn't know the day of your visitation" (19:44). It certainly looks as though, for Luke, this is the glory returning.

Gathercole: Yes, in this instance I wouldn't disagree with you.

Wright: But that again means for me that the cross, for Luke, is already being given (what you might call) a Johannine explanation. In John, when Jesus is "lifted up," he is revealing the divine glory. This is, I think, the seventh sign in John. (There is a sequence of signs, starting with the water into wine, where Jesus reveals his glory, and then the final sign—when Jesus is glorified with a capital *G*, if you like—is on the cross.) Again, we haven't talked about that. Inevitably, perhaps, we've tended to focus on Paul, because when you get a bunch of people from our various traditions—saving your presence, Ma'am [to Edith Humphrey]—within this sort of context, we tend just to go to Paul. But John, and indeed 1 Peter, would have had some interesting stuff to say.

Gathercole: Yes. I think we've had a fair amount of agreement. I think one thing that remains a sticking point is the explanation of the Gospel in terms of the restoration of creation. I'd happily confess (confess in the positive sense, not confess in the reluctant sense!) that God's entire work of redemption consists in the restoration of creation as well. But the primary focus in some of the passages that Doug Moo pointed out, and in some of the passages that I pointed out, the primary focus of God's reconciling activity is with human beings. I'm still stuck on that. I don't know how we'd resolve it.

Wright: Well, I will pray for you, Simon. [Audience laughs.]

Gathercole: Of course, you can eventually get, by a lot of convoluted footwork, from John 3:16 to the restoration of creation, but you have to do a lot of controversial weaving to get there.

Wright: I think it's not controversial. Right at the beginning in Genesis 1 we have a statement that when God makes this strange, extraordinary world, a world that is other than himself, there is a clear statement of how he is going to organize it. He is going to organize it through human beings: he gives to his image-bearers the tasks of looking after the garden, making things happen, being fruitful and multiplying; then, in the next chapter, naming the animals, and so on. To repeat something I said before, among the many things that Genesis 1 and 2 tell me about God is the fact that the One God who deserves the word "God" is a working-through-humans God. That's who he determines to be, and I think there is a deep christological reason for that. We didn't quite have that discussion yesterday; but when God made the world, he made it so that it would be utterly appropriate for his own second self (if you want to put it like that) to become human, in order to be Lord of creation.

As the result of this understanding, we do not need to suppose that, after the "fall" (whatever we mean by that), God had to scratch his head and reflect that, sadly, the Second Person would now need to become incarnate and do the unpleasant job of redeeming the world. Rather, what happens after the fall (I think) is that this calls forth from the One God a further dimension of the self-giving love, the same love by which creation is made in the first place. And the notion of image-bearingness, of the human creature made to reflect God perfectly into the world, is at the heart of that. So, when the image-bearing people go wrong, then the world gets out of joint, precisely because the humans aren't doing their job. So then, of course, God needs to sort out the humans, to put them right. But Romans 8 is very clear that God sorts out the humans *in order to sort out the whole creation*. Again, this is very clear in Revelation, where the human vocation to be the "royal priesthood" is reaffirmed.

This raises an interesting question. I received an e-mail from somebody in India last night, saying, "If we are to reign on the earth, over whom will we reign?" Will it just be nonhuman animals, plants, and so on in God's new world? What will this mean? In my tradition, we sing hymns about resting and reigning with God in heaven, where the reigning has no content whatever. It's just sitting around, being happy to have a crown on. But the question then remains.

Gathercole: That's part of the difficulty, though: because the theme of reigning is so underdeveloped [in the NT], it's hard to see what precise content it has. I totally agree with you on Romans 8, but that's quite an unusual part. It's not what Paul regularly talks about in Romans. I made exactly the same point in my review of your *Paul and the Faithfulness of God.* You like big pictures, so the bigger the picture, the better. I think the danger is that if you focus on the whole sphere, as it were, then there is a danger of missing what is in the center.

Wright: Yes, but I would also refer to 1 Corinthians 15:20–28. This takes us back to our conversation yesterday. It is very interesting to me that when Paul says, at the beginning of the chapter, that "the Messiah died for our sins in accordance with the Scriptures," he continues the argument twenty verses later with a catena of scriptural quotations, which are about the Messiah as the one who *has won* a victory and *will win* a victory. It seems, then, that there is this implicit, very close link between messianic victory and messianic dying for our sins, and the one is the means of the other (compare Gal. 1:4!). The point, then, is that ultimately God will be all in all, which brings us back to exactly the same place, albeit in a different idiom, that we find in Romans 8.

Gathercole: Sure. I agree with that. That is where it ultimately leads to. It is interesting what Paul identifies as of first importance in his summary of the gospel, that Christ died for our sins according to the Scriptures and was raised again from the dead. We could go on about this for hours.

Wright: It is really important that Paul is talking about the center of history. He is talking about events that have happened and are the fulcrum, the hinge around which the great door of history turns, if you like. This is part of the question of the cross in history. In the book I referred to last night, the new *T&T Clark Companion to Atonement*, edited by Adam Johnson, there is a short essay on Bultmann's understanding of the cross. It's very interesting that the author, even though he is a Bultmann fan, needs to say that Bultmann doesn't have very much to contribute on the meaning of the cross. Isn't that interesting? It was just, for Bultmann, in German, the *Dass*: the sheer fact, the event, the thing that had happened. There is very little attempt to interpret or explain why, in Bultmann's own understanding, Jesus' crucifixion should have any particular significance. To me, this seems to be a major Achilles' heel for somebody who is supposed to be a Pauline and a Johannine scholar, one who indeed stands so firmly in the Lutheran tradition.

Gathercole: It's apparently sort of a vertical event without any horizontal extension.

Wright: But that, of course, goes with a much larger problem. It's not that Bultmann was out on a limb. A good deal of early twentieth-century theology simply didn't know what to do, theologically, with history, with historical events, historical narratives, or historical investigation. To this [issue] I want to say, "Put the cross at the middle of it, and you will see that everything else comes into shape."

Gathercole: Yes, I agree on that part. Are we going to have any Q and A?

Wright: If there is anyone who is burning to ask something or say something, I would say, Please do. While you are thinking, I was just going to say two things. One is that I've written a lot about the cross over the years, and I've always found it a spiritual challenge. On this, I would say to anyone here: if you are preaching about the cross, teaching about the cross, leading a Sunday school class, then get friends to pray for you, and make sure you are, as it were, taking appropriate steps to guard against attack. This doctrine, this fact, this world-shaking historical event, is contested territory. This is why it is always controversial, why indeed Christian theology is always controversial.

Gathercole: It is interesting that C. S. Lewis always said he never felt so spiritually dry about a doctrine as when he had just defended it.

Wright: Yes. In my experience over the years, it's been true of talking about the cross, again and again. And I just observe that when I lecture on it.

So now, is anyone bursting to say something? We won't go on indefinitely, but simply if there are one or two urgent things.

Question #14: So, Dr. Wright, could you explain your interpretation of how you think Paul is working out the relationship between the covenant and Romans 2:13? And Dr. Gathercole, if you agree with him or disagree with him, could you give what you think are the implications of his answer? I know that, earlier, Dr. Horton and Dr. Moo both kind of glossed over this text, and both of you sort of chuckled.

Wright: This is a point of considerable detail. I suspect that not everyone in the hall has Romans 2 in their heads. It is one of the harder passages. Romans is a difficult book, and this is one of the difficult bits within it, because the role of chapter 2 as a whole is controversial. Paul is basically saying [that] God is going to judge the whole world, whether or not people have the law. But in 2:13 it isn't those who hear the law who are righteous before God but those who do the law who will be justified. Now, people have said, "Oh, my goodness, here is Paul affirming justification by law-keeping." The answer is that he is here talking about *final justification*. This is not in conflict, then, with what he says in Romans 3:21–26, which is about *present justification*. The point of the gospel is that, at the end, God will put the whole world to right, and that this *future* event has been decisively launched through the *present* achievement of Jesus. God is going to sort out the whole creation, just as Psalms and Isaiah and so on promised he would. In the present time, through the gospel, *God puts people right so that they can be part of his putting-right project for the world*. This inaugurated eschatology is absolutely vital. So when Paul is talking about what happens in the present time, the gospel verdict is issued simply on the basis of faith. One is declared *dikaios* (righteous/just) in the present; but that always, as in Philippians 1:6, anticipates the verdict of the last day. Paul returns to the question of the last-day verdict in Romans 8. It is not true that he expounds "justification" in Romans 1–4 and then something different in chapters 5–8. In Romans 8 he comes back to the *future* verdict, to explain how it is that the *present* verdict of 3:21–31 makes sense as a true anticipation of the *future* verdict of the last day. The people who are on their way to that final verdict are the people who, as in Romans 8:12–17, "are debtors, not to the flesh, to live according to the flesh," because they are to be "led by the Spirit." They are the suffering-to-be-glorified "children of God."

Thus Romans 2 means what it means within a larger eschatological scheme. It in no way is undermined by, or would undermine, justification by faith, which is about the verdict of the gospel in the present.

Gathercole: There is a lovely place in Calvin's commentary where he describes those who argue that 2:13 ["Doers of the law will be justified"] contradicts 3:20, "No one is justified by works of the law": they deserve to be laughed at by schoolboys [laughs]. I think that I broadly agree. Some take it to be hypothetical. I can see the force of the argument, but I tend to go in the other direction. It's not that people are declared righteous on the last day *because* of their deeds; it's *in accordance* with their deeds, not because of their deeds. But the totality of life lived—the direction of travel of the one who is justified by faith, as Tom has said—[amounts to] "putting to death by the Spirit [the works of the law"; Rom. 8:13]; the Spirit, as you see, is crucial.

Wright: It's the work of the Spirit. But again and again, as Paul himself says, "I labored more mightily than they all, yet it was not I but the grace of God that was with me" [1 Cor. 15:10]. That's the odd thing about the Spirit's work. We are required to work; we are not passengers. And yet, we ascribe all the glory and gratitude to the Spirit for doing it in and through us.

Gathercole: Our identity is outside of ourselves; that's how it works. And this is obviously not any sort of sinless perfection. Romans 2 defines it as "those who seek glory and honor and immortality" (2:7).

Wright: Yes, I think we are on the same page here. Sorry, Doug. [laughs]

Question #15: So, naturally we talk a lot about the cross and the work of Christ, but I wanted to ask for just your thoughts on his public ministry and the purpose of it. What would you say to somebody who thought part of Jesus' public ministry was about trying to get himself killed to be a sacrifice?

Wright: "Trying to get himself killed"? It is, of course, always possible to describe Jesus' motivation in such a way, yet as Ed Sanders said in *Jesus and Judaism*,[1] that would just make him seem "weird." It wasn't that Jesus was "trying to get himself killed." He needs to announce and launch the king-dom of God. And Jesus knew, because he knew the Psalms and Isaiah and Daniel like he knew the back of his hand, that this vocation would involve him going straight to the place where the darkness was doing its worst and then taking its full force upon himself. That's what the agony in Gethsemane is all

---

1. E. [Edward] P. Sanders, *Jesus and Judaism* (Philadelphia: Fortress Press, 1985), 333.

about, I think, and that's why Jesus says, "Watch and pray so that you don't enter the *peirasmos*, the time of testing" [Mark 14:38 and par.]. It's a vocational thing. Zechariah as well is hugely important for Jesus at that moment, though it's a very difficult book for us to reappropriate [cf. 12:19]. And this is simply Jesus' vocation. It was, of course, a strange vocation, from which he shrank but to which he was obedient. So, I think that is quite clear.

And I think this is evident from the very beginning. In Matthew's story, it's evident from the start when old Herod is out to kill Jesus. It's there early on in Mark [3:6], when the Herodians and the Pharisees—there's an unlikely pairing—get together to plot against him. It's going on all the time. It isn't the case that Jesus had a delightfully happy time earlier in his public career, and then at a certain point he said to himself, "Actually, I've got to go to Jerusalem and die." Jesus was doing and announcing the kingdom from the start, and this was always contested and dangerous. And he went to the place where the contest and the danger was at its fiercest.

Gathercole: I think a passage that helped me understand this, when I was a student, was the dialogue between Jesus and John the Baptist's envoys in Matthew 11, where John the Baptist sends a message with a question, "Are you the one who is to come, or should we wait for someone else?" And Jesus says, "Well, go back and tell John what you have seen. The blind see. The lame walk. The lepers are cleansed. The deaf hear. The dead are raised, and the poor have the good news preached to them" [11:2–6]. With the coming of the Messiah, who is the king of the kingdom, the kingdom starts taking shape. These healings are not just evidence that Jesus is the Messiah; they also are signs that the kingdom is coming and being inaugurated.

Wright: The inauguration of the reign of God. Yes! Does that help? Okay. Thank you.

Question #16: First of all, I would like to thank you and all the guests here. I did want to ask how your ecclesial tradition and background have shaped this subject of study and even generally [have shaped] other subjects of study. As an Anglican myself, I can see how that would affect, let's say, the end of Luke, and how we see that their eyes aren't opened until after Word *and* sacrament.

Wright: The first time I sang anything in a choir, I was seven years old. I was singing in the Ripieno Choir with a performance of Bach's *St. Matthew Passion*, at the parish church in the town where I grew up. In those days, even a small town could put on that kind of thing. I was hugely formed from an early age by the *Matthew Passion* and by Handel's *Messiah*. I first met many of the great biblical texts as music, as something I could *participate in*, long before I ever dreamed of studying them as history or as an academic or whatever, so I sensed what they meant because the music was telling me. From there it was and has been a lifelong delight, without leaving the music behind, to explore the texts themselves. But I came in on the ground floor with music, and, of course, with the hymnody, such as "O Sacred Head, Now Wounded" or "When I Survey the Wondrous Cross." One of things I worry about today is the number of people in our livelier, bouncier churches who just don't sing the old hymns at all. That's a real problem since they are foundational for so many of us as ways of coming to sense and appropriate for ourselves the meaning of this.

Gathercole: Yes, when you said you came in on the ground floor, I think I came in through the back door. I was a horrible little pagan. I remember, when I was at boarding school, being taken on Sundays to the local Anglican church. And you know the wording better than I do. You're sent out as living sacrifices to do the work of God: that is how you are ushered out at the end. And I remember thinking, "I don't want to be a living sacrifice, thank you very much." [Everyone laughs.] But when I became a Christian as a teenager, I was gradually informed partly through reading the Scripture and partly through singing those wonderful old hymns that you mentioned.

Wright: Yes, it is very informative. Last question, ma'am.

Question #17: Yesterday, during the first point-counterpoint session and after Dr. Gathercole asked you how Gentiles are saved, I believe you answered, "Through the defeat of idols through the work of the cross." Am I correct? [Wright nods.] All right. I was a little confused by that simply because we have, throughout the Old Testament, the witness of multiple Gentiles coming to faith and converting to Judaism. We also have, within the neighboring communities, the presence of a large number of God-fearers who have converted to Judaism in some measure. Also in the Old Testament narratives, we repeatedly have God almost laughingly despising the power and worship of the idols, as common in neighboring countries. So I am curious [about] how those play into this concept of the defeat of idols.

Wright: Of course, there are numerous exceptions, whether it's Ruth or Rahab, or the Ninevites when Jonah goes and preaches, or whatever. So, all that stuff happens. But the point is actually, as 1 John says, "The whole world lies in the power of the evil one" [5:19]. Now, there is some tension between whether you say that's not the case anymore, or whether it's still in some sense the case until Christ returns. But I was really starting from John 12 and working out [Jesus' saying] that "the ruler of this age" is driven out when Jesus is "lifted up" [12:31–32]. It is as though the people you mention in the Old Testament, who come as God-fearers or whatever, are foretastes of that new reality; but it's always a kind of anomaly. Yet what Paul celebrates is that *now there is no anomaly*: Gentiles can come in, because now the promise is fulfilled, which is the Davidic promise. God has reclaimed the whole world through the Messiah's victory. We didn't talk about this earlier, but [all this is based on the belief that] the Abrahamic promise is extended through Psalm 2 in a very dramatic way, when God says to the Messiah in Psalm 2, "Ask of me and I'll give you"—not just one strip of territory, but—"*the nations* as your possession, the uttermost parts of the earth as your inheritance" [2:8]. In other words, Abraham was given this small bit of territory [Canaan, Gen. 17:8] as an advance statement, so that it was always anomalous when other people were allowed to come in [or stay in]—Gentiles, in other words, who adhered to Israel. But now, since the achievement of Jesus, you don't have to do that [be in that land]. Now the creator God will be with you wherever you are. Something has happened (in other words): as a result the whole world is a different place. There is a sense of ontological change. Of course, this doesn't mean that all Gentiles are automatically saved. They are not. The gospel must be preached to them. But that's when the mystery happens. Paul and the other apostles and evangelists announce the gospel, and the Spirit works powerfully through the preaching of the Word. Some people hate it and throw stones. Others find that it has transformed them, and they form a totally new sort of community. Yes, it's a new sort of community, over against even the best sort of potential polychrome community that you might have had in the pre-Christian Jewish world. So there is indeed a radical newness with the gospel; but that doesn't discount the many previous exceptions. Are you on board with all that, Simon?

Gathercole: Yes. I'm not sure if there are even exceptions since new worshipers of the God of Israel, such as Ruth and Rahab, did not cease to be Moabites or Jerichoites. They have an allegiance to Israel but don't become Israelites. Similarly, in Paul's day, those who converted to Judaism, going the whole hog and getting circumcised and all that, were called "proselytes," which translates the term *prosēlytai* [e.g., Matt. 23:15; Acts 2:10], used in the Greek Old Testament for resident aliens [e.g., 1 Chron. 22:2 LXX]. So they were in that category rather than necessarily being full children of Abraham in the whole sense.

Wright: But I think the crucial thing about all this, to come back and summarize the whole conversation really, is that, with the death of the one who is then raised from the dead, something has happened as a result of which the world is a radically different place. I think we all basically agree with that. In other words, this isn't just opening up a possibility. It isn't just one more revelation of the fact that God loves people, and so on. It's actually about the fact that the world has changed, and we are thereby commissioned to be agents of that change. Does that make sense?

Further Reading

COMPILED BY ROBERT B. STEWART

In theology there is no substitute for reading the primary sources. Inevitably secondary literature simplifies the issues. This is no criticism of secondary sources but rather a necessary consequence of their purpose. The descriptions in this list are not exempt from that reality. No claim is made that there are no other significant works that could have profitably been included. This bibliography is intended to be an aid to readers, especially but not only for students and nonspecialists. The hope is that these annotations will prove useful. Most of the time I merely summarize the contents, but at times I offer some personal opinions. They are just that, my own opinions. The "Classics Works" are arranged in chronological order. The "Other Sources" are listed alphabetically by the author's last name, whose relevant works (if more than one) are then listed chronologically.

Classic Works on the Atonement

Athanasius of Alexandria. *On the Incarnation.* In *Nicene and Post-Nicene Fathers.* Second Series, vol. 4. Edited by Philip Schaff and Henry Wace. Translated by Archibald Robertson. Buffalo: Christian Literature Publishing Co., 1892. Reprint, Peabody, MA: Hendrickson Publishers, 1994.

In this wide-ranging (4th-century) work on the reasons for the incarnation, which is a classic example of both Christology from above and Christocentrism, Athanasius puts forward a Recapitulation Theory of the atonement; Christ came to obey where Adam disobeyed, to restore what Adam corrupted, which results in *theōsis*.

Anselm of Canterbury. *Why God Became Man*. In *The Major Works*. Edited by Brian Davies and G. R. Evans. New York: Oxford University Press, 1998.

Cur Deus Homo, the original Latin title, was written in 1099 and is the first sustained treatment of the atonement in Christian history. In many ways this is the model that all other later works must take into consideration. Often caricatured as a work picturing God as a petty feudal lord, this work actually has *justice*, which demands either punishment or satisfaction, as its foremost concern, along with explaining the divine motivation behind the incarnation. Quite possibly the greatest book on the atonement in Christian history.

Abelard, Peter. *Commentary on the Epistle to the Romans*. Translated by Steven Cartwright. Washington, DC: Catholic University of America Press, 2011.

Often held up in secondary literature as the model Moral Example theorist concerning the reason for Christ's death, Abelard (12th century) is more than that. More than one contemporary theologian has tried to exonerate Abelard of this charge. Abelard clearly thinks that the *result* of Christ's death is that the faithful are moved to follow his example, but it is difficult to locate a passage clearly teaching that this is the *reason* for Christ's death. Abelard opposed Anselm's satisfaction theory because he thought it immoral.

Calvin, John. *Institutes of the Christian Religion*. 2 vols. Translated by Henry Beveridge. London: James Clarke, 1962.

In book 2, chapters 12–17, one finds Calvin's treatment of the atonement (16th century). Calvin presents a more tightly reasoned, scripturally supported version of penal substitution than does Luther, in that Calvin's view is tightly tied to justification and union with Christ, both of which come only by faith.

Socinus, Faustus. *De Jesu Christo Servatore*. In *Bibliotheca Fratrum Polonorum* II. Edited by Andreas Wissowatius. Amsterdam, 1668.

Socinus was a rigorous and determined opponent of both Anselm's satisfaction theory and the magisterial Reformers's penal substitution theory. This work was a serious and sustained project, to which Grotius and others could not fail to respond.

Grotius, Hugo. *A Defence of the Catholic Faith concerning the Satisfaction of Christ, against Faustus Socinus*. Translated by Frank Hugh Foster. Andover, MA: Warren F. Draper, 1889.

A response to Socinus's denial of penal substitution, Grotius's position is generally referred to as the Governmental Theory. Grotius (early 17th century) is often pictured in secondary literature as denying penal substitution. Although there is no hint of imputation in this work, there is more than one place where penal substitution is affirmed. Uniquely, Grotius pictures God not as a judge, who must follow the law, but as a ruler, who can make or relax laws. Christ dies as an innocent, willing man in place of willing sinners because of the love of God, but not in contradiction to the justice of God. Some think that Grotius veered too close to Socinus and ended up affirming some of what he meant to deny.

Turretin, Francis. *Institutes of Elenctic Theology*. 3 vols. Translated by George Musgrave Giger. Edited by James T. Dennison Jr. Phillipsburg, NJ: P&R, 1992, 1994, 1997.

Comprehensive statement of late seventeenth-century Reformed theology. Written in scholastic form, Question 14, on "The Mediatorial Office of Christ," gives significant attention to the atonement. In contrast to Socinus, special attention is given to the necessity of divine justice. To my knowledge this is the first work to use the term "penal substitution," although others had certainly taught the idea. This work was especially influential for both the Puritans and the old Princeton Theology (1812–1920s).

Campbell, John McLeod. *The Nature of the Atonement and Its Relation to Remission of Sins and Eternal Life*. London: Macmillan, 1869.

Highly significant late nineteenth-century work in which Campbell closely ties incarnation to atonement, as well as stresses not only that Christ suffered for sins, but also that Christ saw sin and sinners through God's (loving) eyes and thus was able genuinely to feel sorrow for sinners. Important in that Campbell moves away from penal substitution, or at least from Hodge's understanding of penal substitution.

Aulén, Gustav. *Christus Victor: An Historical Study of the Three Main Types of the Idea of the Atonement*. Translated by A. G. Herbert. London: SPCK, 1931.

Enormously influential book (1930 in Swedish) that has literally impacted the way the atonement is talked about by theologians and historians. In the form of a historical study, this work argues that the dominant patristic view was that Christ's death was primarily intended to provide victory over evil spiritual powers. Since its publication, any view that has a similar thesis is generally referred to as a *Christus Victor* view.

Barth, Karl. *Church Dogmatics*. Vol. IV, *The Doctrine of Reconciliation*. Edinburgh: T&T Clark, 1988.

As in all things Barth, this (1956–67) four-part work is a forthrightly Trinitarian treatment of the atonement. Significantly, God the Father suffers in sending the Son to redeem fallen humanity. There is also more than a touch of a recapitulation theory to Barth's position. This work prompted a host of others, such as Balthasar, Rahner, Jüngel, Moltmann, and Fiddes, to build upon and modify his position.

Other Sources

Atkinson, William P. *The "Spiritual Death" of Jesus: A Pentecostal Investigation*. Boston: Brill, 2009.

Book publication of Atkinson's dissertation critiquing an idea popularly taught by "Word-Faith" teachers and televangelists, holding that Jesus took on satanic nature and died spiritually, then was reborn in hell. Importantly, it distinguishes between classical Pentecostalism and Word-Faith doctrine.

Baker, Mark D., and Joel B. Green. *Recovering the Scandal of the Cross: Atonement in New Testament and Contemporary Contexts*. Downers Grove, IL: InterVarsity Press, 2003.

This book studies the variety of biblical pictures of the atonement found in the New Testament. Specifically, it asks the question of whether penal substitutionary atonement is grounded in Scripture or in culture.

Beilby, James, and Paul R. Eddy, eds. *The Nature of the Atonement: Four Views*. Spectrum Multiview Book. Downers Grove, IL: InterVarsity Academic, 2006.

This book is a must for anyone interested in the doctrine of the atonement. Limited in breadth in that only four positions are addressed, it still is an excellent primer on the major positions that have been held on the doctrine. Especially helpful in that the advocate for each view offers a summary statement, to which the other three offer respectful critiques. One concern is that the choice of positions represented seems uneven. That the Christus Victor and Penal Substitution models must be included seems obvious; the Kaleidoscope view, albeit a somewhat unusual name, also seems fitting, but was the Healing View really important enough for the Satisfaction View not to be included? Still, well worth the time and price.

Bellinger, William H., and William R. Farmer, eds. *Jesus and the Suffering Servant: Isaiah 53 and Christian Origins*. Harrisburg, PA: Trinity Press, 1998.

Important book of essays by top scholars on one of the most important Old Testament passages concerning the atonement. Of particular significance are two essays by Daniel Bailey, "Concepts of *Stellvertretung* in the Interpretation of Isaiah 53" and "Suffering Servant: Recent Tübingen Scholarship on Isaiah 53." Also of interest is the essay by Morna Hooker and the response by Mikeal Parsons. Interestingly, one can also see some of N. T. Wright's earlier thinking on the atonement in his concluding article.

Boersma, Hans. *Violence, Hospitality, and the Cross: Reappropriating the Atonement Tradition*. Grand Rapids: Baker Academic, 2004.

Broad in its coverage of issues related to the atonement, this book by a Reformed theologian interacting with postmodernists—especially Derrida and Girard, concerning violence—finds their concern legitimate but their proposals inadequate. Interestingly, Boersma puts forward the idea of recapitulation as the means to unite the concepts of Christus Victor, substitution, and moral example, all of which have some legitimacy. Interesting and helpful book.

Boyd, Gregory A. *The Crucifixion of the Warrior God: Interpreting the Old Testament's Violent Portraits of God in Light of the Cross*. 2 vols. Minneapolis: Fortress Press, 2017.

A massive argument for seeing the cross as a call to nonviolence. Arguing for a cruciform hermeneutic, Boyd consciously follows Origen in arguing that all biblical passages stating that God actively and violently judges are in fact accommodations (thus allegorical), while accounts of judgment via divine withdrawal are actual and accurate descriptions. This self-affirming hermeneutic is woefully insufficient, in my view.

Chalke, Steve, and Alan Mann. *The Lost Message of Jesus*. Grand Rapids: Zondervan, 2004.

This book, released in 2003, created a firestorm of controversy and birthed a number of books, articles, and at least one conference, either criticizing or praising it. Largely coming from the perspective of the so-called Emergent Church, this book intends to recover lost elements of the gospel that Jesus preached. At times it does; at other times, it does not.

Craig, William Lane. *The Atonement*. Elements in the Philosophy of Religion. Cambridge: Cambridge University Press, 2018.

Useful little book that covers biblical, historical, and philosophical issues concerning the atonement in a succinct but significant way. It also corrects some frequent stereotypes concerning several historical figures. Whatever position one takes, this book should be read.

Crisp, Oliver D., and Fred Sanders, eds. *Locating Atonement: Explorations in Constructive Dogmatics*. Proceedings of the Los Angeles Theology Conference. Grand Rapids: Zondervan, 2015.

A collection of wide-ranging essays from an interdisciplinary team of scholars, this book records the proceedings of the 2015 Los Angeles Theology Conference. An example of top-notch contemporary Christian scholarship that goes beyond arguing for one position on the atonement over against another: it tries to place the atonement in relation to other theological concepts and our contemporary cultural situation.

Dever, Mark J., Ligon Duncan III, R. Albert Mohler Jr., and C. J. Mahaney. *Proclaiming a Cross-Centered Theology*. Together for the Gospel. Wheaton, IL: Crossway, 2009.

The fruit of the 2008 "Together for the Gospel" conference, this is a volume of sermons and lectures intended for ministers and interested laity. Throughout, it is a defense of the Reformation doctrine of penal substitutionary atonement. The tone is at times polemical because the authors' shared concern is that the gospel is at risk because "the atonement is being misconceived and mistaught in too many evangelical books and churches."

Dodd, C. H. *The Apostolic Preaching and Its Developments*. London: Hodder and Stoughton, 1964.

Important book, written in 1936 by a colossus of biblical scholarship, arguing that the term "propitiation" had no place in the New Testament. Dodd's preferred translation of *hilastērion* (Rom. 3:25) was "expiation." That explanation was widely interpreted as an outright denial of penal substitution.

Forsyth, P. T. *Positive Preaching and the Modern Mind*. London: Hodder & Stoughton, 1908.
———. *The Cruciality of the Cross*. 1909. Carlisle, UK: Paternoster, 1997.
———. *The Work of Christ: Studies in the Sacrifice and Character of Jesus Christ, and the Symbolism of the Cross in Christianity*. 1910. London: Independent Press, 1938.

These works by a pastor-preacher extraordinaire demonstrate how one early twentieth-century thinker emphasized both penal substitution, the incarnation, and Chalcedonian Christology, thus attempting to bring together the respective emphases of evangelicalism (penal substitution), liberalism (incarnation), and Chalcedonian Christology (two natures).

Frey, Jörg, and Jens Schröter, eds. *Deutungen des Todes Jesu im Neuen Testament*. 2nd, rev. ed. Tübingen: Mohr Siebeck, 2012.

Despite the title, this volume (English: Interpretations of the Death of Jesus in the New Testament) contains a number of technical but important essays, not only on how the death of Jesus was understood in the New Testament but also in Judaism and in the ancient Greco-Roman world.

Gathercole, Simon. *Defending Substitution: An Essay on Atonement in Paul*. Acadia Studies in Bible and Theology. Grand Rapids: Baker Academic, 2015.

Fabulous little book that is a gold mine of information on views that oppose the concept of substitution in the atonement, as well as a fair-minded counterargument. Gathercole recognizes good points from positions he ultimately disagrees with, supports the concept of substitution, and shows some places in the Pauline corpus that undergird his position. Yet Gathercole concludes that one need not separate substitution, representation, and liberation from one

another; nor need one understand Christ's death just to pay either
for sins or Sin. These features can and should fit together.

Gese, Hartmut. *Essays on Biblical Theology.* Translated by Keith Crim.
Eugene, OR: Wipf & Stock, 2012.

Wide-ranging book of essays by Gese, but section 4, on the
atonement, is of particular interest. Gese argues here, and in other
writings, that rather than being a substitute for sinful Israel, Christ
takes the place of Israel (German: *Stellvertretung*), as an animal
did when being sacrificed, and symbolically brings Israel into the
presence of God, thus reconciling Israel to God. The death of Christ
functions in the same way.

Girard, René. *Things Hidden since the Foundation of the World.*
Translated by Stephen Bann and Michael Metteer. 1978 in French.
Stanford, CA: Stanford University Press, 1987.
———. *I See Satan Fall Like Lightning.* Translated by James G.
Williams. 1999 in French. Maryknoll, NY: Orbis Books, 2001.

Interesting literary and anthropological works arguing that Jesus
died to put an end to societal "scapegoating." As such, the cross was
an example of injustice being propagated against an innocent party.
Girard sees Jesus' death not as a sacrifice to God that saves us, but
rather as a means of saving us from sacrifice. Girard's work, along
with Wink's and Boyd's, contribute to the "atonement as an end to
violence" model of the atonement.

Green, Joel B., and Mark D. Baker. *Recovering the Scandal of the Cross:
Atonement in New Testament and Contemporary Contexts.* Downers
Grove, IL: IVP Academic, 2000.

Clearly written book that proves useful for both specialists and
nonspecialists and includes not only careful exploration of relevant
biblical texts and a historical survey of major views, but also reports
ways in which the atonement has been understood by feminists and
in various global cultures. Understood by some as an attempt to
undermine penal substitution.

Grensted, Laurence W. *A Short History of the Doctrine of the Atonement.*
London: Longmans, Green & Co., 1920.

Older serious study regarding the history of the doctrine of the
atonement. This work especially gives significant attention to this
doctrine in the early church. One nice touch is that in the footnotes

one finds quotations in the original language matching English translations given in the body.

Gunton, Colin E. *The Actuality of Atonement: A Study of Metaphor, Rationality, and the Christian Tradition.* Grand Rapids: Wm. B. Eerdmans Publishing Co., 1989.

Significant technical work on metaphor and the atonement. Gunton posits that we use metaphors to express what is real or actual. Assesses the work of several significant historical voices concerning the atonement and argues that no single interpretation of the cross does justice to all that the cross represents. Concludes that understanding the atonement demands living it as well. Not for theological novices.

Jeffery, Steve, Michael Ovey, and Andrew Sach. *Pierced for Our Transgressions: Rediscovering the Glory of Penal Substitution.* Wheaton, IL: Crossway, 2007.

A systematic case for penal substitutionary atonement. The authors go beyond reactionary criticism of those who would challenge their view (although, quite logically, there is some of that) to present a positive historical, biblical/exegetical, theological, and cultural case for their view.

Johnson, Adam, ed. *T&T Clark Companion to Atonement.* London: Bloomsbury Publishing, 2017.

Massive collection of mostly accessible articles on over one hundred subjects related to the atonement. With some exceptions, the articles mostly focus on theological topics and historical figures of significance for the study of the atonement, leaving one to look elsewhere for exegetical detail. A bit pricey but quite useful, especially for theologians and historians.

McKnight, Scot. *A Community Called Atonement.* Nashville: Abingdon Press, 2007.

Wide-ranging, interesting book that touches on many subjects and recognizes the need for multiple metaphors to express fully the purpose of Jesus' death. The central idea is that Jesus identified with sinful humans and thus died for them, with them, and instead of them. Identification leads to incorporation into Christ, which leads to a repaired relationship with God and one another in order to restore the image of God. McKnight effectively shifts the atonement from soteriology to ecclesiology.

Moltmann, Jürgen. *The Crucified God.* London: SCM Press, 1974.

In a book mostly about theodicy, Moltmann offers a panentheistic Trinitarian atonement that serves the purpose of revealing the suffering of God both as Son and as Father, through which the world is changed. As a result, faith is protected from both (non-Trinitarian) monotheism and atheism as the cross becomes the inaugurating moment of God's eschatological future. Throughout this book are themes of social liberation and the rejection of an immutable and impassible God.

Morris, Leon. *The Apostolic Preaching of the Cross.* London: Tyndale Press, 1955.

This book, based on Morris's dissertation, was largely perceived to be a response to Dodd. Morris analyzed several biblical and theological subjects by careful work in the Greek. He gave separate chapters to "Redemption," "Covenant," "The Blood," "The Lamb of God," "Propitiation," "Reconciliation," and "Justification." Morris included two chapters on "Propitiation" and two on "Justification." In the two chapters on "Propitiation," Morris frequently challenges Dodd's position.

Pinnock, Clark H., and Robert C. Brow. *Unbounded Love: A Good News Theology for the 21st Century.* Downers Grove, IL: InterVarsity Press, 1994.

This book, which was a continuation of Pinnock's project of Open Theism, seeks to recast Christian systematic theology around the theme of love. Every chapter includes a subtitle with an adjective modifying the word "Love." In the chapter on atonement, Pinnock and Brow put forward a subjective atonement: Jesus died to change our attitude toward God.

Pugh, Ben. *Atonement Theories: A Way through the Maze.* Eugene, OR: Cascade Books, 2014.

Very useful little book that grew out of a short-term course that Pugh taught for Mattersey Hall (UK). Rich theologically and historically, the book treats several figures, particularly Pentecostal theologians, who are not normally included in survey books. Mainline theologians take a myopic viewpoint when they overlook the contributions, both positively and negatively, that Pentecostals have made to atonement theology. The most up-to-date book of its type. This book is an excellent resource.

Ray, Darby Kathleen. *Deceiving the Devil: Atonement, Abuse, and Ransom.* Cleveland: Pilgrim Press, 1998.

Ray argues for a reworked and demythologized version of the Christus Victor theory, a version that takes seriously feminist and liberationist perspectives. A useful book from a feminist perspective, positing that traditional views of the cross implicitly sanction violence against women, as do other forms of passivity in the face of violence.

Rutledge, Fleming. *The Crucifixion: Understanding the Death of Christ.* Grand Rapids: Wm. B. Eerdmans Publishing Co., 2017.

Massive, elegantly written book arguing that Jesus was crucified primarily to defeat the powers of Sin, Death, and the Law. While not denying the importance of individual sins, the focus is upon Sin—an active, malevolent agency bent on despoiling and undoing what God is doing in this world. Penal substitutionary atonement is downplayed if not denied altogether. Universalism is at least implied. Apocalyptic deliverance is at the heart of Jesus' mission.

Simpson, A. B. *The Gospel of Healing.* New York: Christian Alliance Press, [1880].

Classic text arguing that physical healing is included in the atonement. Sickness is not part of creation but rather an effect of the fall; as such it has a spiritual cause and therefore needs a spiritual cure. Health is therefore as much a spiritual right for the faithful as is forgiveness and righteousness. Note well: Simpson does not advocate Word-Faith positive confession, but rather an expanded penal substitution position.

Stott, John R. W. *The Cross of Christ.* Downers Grove, IL: InterVarsity Press, 1986.

A robust defense of penal substitution that also addresses broader issues in Christology, as well as the problem of suffering. Stott maintains that God is perfectly loving and perfectly consistent. Sounding like Anselm at points, Stott bases substitution within a Trinitarian theology and on God's need for self-satisfaction to be consistent with his loving and just nature.

Tidball, Derek, David Hilborn, and Justin Thacker, eds. *The Atonement Debate: Papers from the London Symposium on the Theology of Atonement.* Grand Rapids: Zondervan, 2008.

This book includes the papers from a conference dealing with *The Lost Message of Jesus* and features a stellar list of authors, such as I. H. Marshall, Joel Green, Oliver Crisp, and Stephen Holmes, to name but a few. Significantly, it includes Steve Chalke.

Wink, Walter. *Naming the Powers: The Language of Power in the New Testament*. Philadelphia: Fortress Press, 1984.
————. *Unmasking the Powers: The Invisible Forces That Determine Human Existence*. Philadelphia: Fortress Press, 1986.
————. *Engaging the Powers: Discernment and Resistance in a World of Domination*. Minneapolis: Fortress Press, 1992.

This trilogy identifies Pauline principalities and powers primarily as human systems that oppress through violence and financial manipulation. The cross exposes these systems and strips them of their power and thus, if not ushering in God's reign, at least making the world ready for the reign of God, which eliminates every form of violence, both on a personal and a corporate level.

Wright, N. T. *The Day the Revolution Began: Reconsidering the Meaning of Jesus's Crucifixion*. San Francisco: HarperOne, 2016.

The book that spawned the fourteenth Greer-Heard Point-Counterpoint Forum, recorded in this present volume. Wright focuses upon the cross as the event that radically changed the world. He places the cross within the big-picture narrative of God's rescuing Israel from exile in order to set the world right, not just to get individuals to heaven. In order to do this, sin—not just as individual acts that break moral codes, but also sin as a vocational failure, the refusal to play our part in God's purposes for his creation—must be addressed and defeated. Wright affirms a version of penal substitution, joined with an apocalyptic-deliverance type of Christus Victor model. Several have reacted strongly against this book, claiming that it denies penal substitution, a claim that Wright strongly denies.

Index

CPSIA information can be obtained
at www.ICGtesting.com
Printed in the USA
LVHW060812140221
679200LV00004B/4

9 780664 265878